South East Asia

Makers
of the
Modern
World

South East Asia
Prince Charoon and others
Andrew Dalby

HH
HAUS HISTORIES

First published in Great Britain in 2010 by
Haus Publishing Ltd
70 Cadogan Place
London SW1X 9AH
www.hauspublishing.com

Copyright © Andrew Dalby, 2010

The moral right of the author has been asserted

A CIP catalogue record for this book
is available from the British Library

ISBN 978-1-905791-85-9

Series design by Susan Buchanan
Typeset in Minion by MacGuru Ltd
Printed in Dubai by Oriental Press

Contents

The Indochina Delegate

'Comrades,' said the thin Vietnamese to applause, 'I wanted to be here today to stand beside you in your work for the world-wide revolution. Instead, in the greatest sadness, in the deepest desolation, I am here to protest, as a socialist, against the abominable crimes committed in my native land. You know that French capitalism arrived in Vietnam fifty years ago. We were conquered at the point of the bayonet and in the name of capitalism'. He repeated the term, to cries of 'Yes! Quite right!' 'Since that day we have been shamefully oppressed and exploited; more than that, we have been horribly butchered and poisoned, and I mean the word literally: poisoned by opium and alcohol. In these few minutes I cannot describe all the atrocities committed in Indochina by capitalist bandits. Our prisons are more numerous than our schools. They never close, and they are full to overflowing … That, comrades, is the treatment reserved for more than twenty million Vietnamese – the equivalent of more than half the population of France. And they are under a French protectorate!' Applause. 'The Socialist Party must act effectively in favour of oppressed native peoples.'

He had the audience on his side. Many at this Congress of the French Socialist Party, at Tours in December 1920, were guiltily aware that for all their egalitarian principles they had done very little for the African and Asian peoples under French rule. The Paris Peace Conference of 1919 had changed nothing in the French colonies: the 'free, open-minded and absolutely impartial adjustment of all colonial claims', promised by President Woodrow Wilson in his Fourteen Points, was irrelevant to territories held by the victorious powers.

The audience's cries of 'Bravo!' were interrupted as Jean Longuet, Socialist deputy, co-founder of *L'Humanité*, grandson of Karl Marx, and vocal critic of the Peace Conference and its derided offspring, the Treaty of Versailles, stood up to defend his personal record. 'I have spoken in Parliament in defence of native peoples!'

'In taking the floor I asserted a dictatorship of silence,' said the Vietnamese to laughter. 'The Socialist Party must make socialist propaganda in every one of the colonies. We will regard adhesion to the Third International as your formal undertaking to accord to colonial questions, at long last, the importance they deserve … we shall be even happier, tomorrow, if the Party will send a socialist comrade to Indochina to investigate our problems at first hand.

'In the name of all humanity, in the name of all socialists, right and left, we say to you: Comrades, be our saviours!'

'The Indochina delegate,' said the chairman, 'will be aware from this applause that the whole Socialist Party is with him in condemning the crimes of the bourgeoisie.' [1]

It was true. Jean Longuet, robbed of the floor by the 'Indochina delegate', was also to be on the losing side when the vote was taken. The French Socialist Party had until this moment been a member of the Second or Workers' International, whose record on anti-colonialism was weak. At this, its 18th congress, the Party voted to affiliate to Lenin's Third or Communist International, which had mocked the 1919 Peace Conference and called for two of its leaders, Georges Clemenceau and David Lloyd George, Prime Ministers of France and Britain, to be 'toppled'.

By this affiliation the French Communist Party was born; and the 'Indochina delegate', the future Hồ Chí Minh, was present at its birth. Another who was present was Agent Devèze of the *Sûreté*. Recalled from retirement to assist with surveillance, he had travelled from Paris on the same train as the Indochina delegate (a three-hour trip by express from the Gare d'Orsay; change at Saint-Pierre-des-Corps; 47 francs each way, second class). On return, Devèze reported fully to Jean Przyluski, a scholarly linguist who had built up the French spy network in southwestern China and was now nearing the end of his secondment to the Paris police. By this time Przyluski had files on 250 Indochinese political agitators and potential dissidents in France;[2] one of the most dangerous, he now believed, was this thin young man with piercing eyes and a scarred left ear, a tuberculosis sufferer as were so many others, currently using the name of Nguyễn Ái Quốc.[3] It was a false name; the policemen were sure of that. Vietnamese, like some other South East Asians, may have a succession of names in the course of their lives, but this custom does not fit the French mould. Almost as much effort was devoted to discovering Nguyễn Ái Quốc's origins and 'real name' as to recording his activities and contacts.

As far as the police were concerned he had burst upon the scene 18 months earlier, on 18 June 1919, and his first known act was quite enough to startle them. He delivered to the Secretariat of the Peace Conference, in the panelled grandeur of

CLAIMS OF THE VIETNAMESE PEOPLE, 18 JUNE 1919
Excellency,
We take the liberty of submitting to you the accompanying memorandum setting forth the claims of the Vietnamese people on the occasion of the Allied victory. We count on your benevolence to honour our appeal with your support whenever opportunity offers.

We beg your Excellency graciously to accept the assurance of our deep respect.

For the Group of Annamite Patriots

[Signed] Nguyen Ai Quac
56, rue Monsieur-le-Prince – Paris

CLAIMS OF THE VIETNAMESE PEOPLE
Since the victory of the Allies, all subject peoples are trembling with hope at the promise of an era of law and justice now in prospect by virtue of the formal and solemn engagements undertaken before the whole world by the various powers of the Entente in the struggle of civilisation against barbarism. As they wait for the nationality principle to pass from the domain of the ideal to that of reality through the effective recognition of the sacred right of peoples to determine their own destiny, the People of the former Empire of Annam, now French Indochina, present to the Noble Governments of the Entente in general and to the honorable French Government in particular the following humble claims:

1) General amnesty for all native political convicts.
2) Reform of Indochinese justice by granting to natives the same judicial guarantees as to Europeans and by total and final suppression of Special Tribunals, instruments of terror and oppression against the most responsible section of the Annamite people.
3) Freedom of the press and of opinion.
4) Freedom to associate and meet.
5) Freedom to emigrate and travel abroad.
6) Freedom of education, and creation in every province of technical and professional schools for the native population.
7) Ending of rule by decree; imposition of the rule of law.

the Quai d'Orsay, typed copies, individually addressed to each official Allied delegation, of a memorial in competent French entitled *Revendications du peuple annamite* ('Claims of the

Vietnamese People'). It bore the address 56, rue Monsieur-le-Prince, not far from the Sorbonne.

The *Revendications* were entered on the Conference record.[4] A few delegations, including the Americans, sent polite acknowledgments; that was all. Such documents arrived frequently. Woodrow Wilson's Fourteen Points had held out the hope to subject peoples that from this Peace Conference would come self-government. As a result, a great many delegations had come to Paris uninvited to lobby for self-government. Most of them took hotel accommodation, enjoyed Paris at their supporters' expense, and were easily watched.

In the case of the Vietnamese, the group was unknown, the signatory was unknown, and the self-government demanded would come (if it were to come at all) at the expense of France. It is no surprise then that, while others did nothing, France took action on receipt of the *Revendications*. Georges Clemenceau, Prime Minister of France, President of the Conference, leader of the French delegation, had received a version that made particular appeal to the noble French people, who 'represent freedom and justice and will never renounce their high ideal of universal brotherhood; thus, in hearing the voice of the oppressed, they will do their duty to France and to humanity'. Clemenceau did not reply to it, but he immediately wrote to his Colonial Minister, Albert Sarraut, newly returned from his second term as Governor-General of Indochina, demanding to know the identity of this 'Nguyen Ai Quac'. Having made initial enquiries, Sarraut was sufficiently intrigued to invite the mysterious claimant to an interview at the Ministry on 6 September.

Sarraut, a philosopher of empire, had himself spoken grandly of a new approach to relations between France and the colonies. His theory of colonialism was characterised by the French word *association* and by the title of his magnum opus to be published in 1923, *La mise en valeur des colonies françaises* ('Putting the French colonies to good use'). British, Dutch and American imperial thinkers of this period developed similar theories of colonialism as partnership; in the 1920s and 1930s such ideas were the foundation for advanced policies and persuasive propaganda. The common opinion in France was that under Sarraut's governorship major reforms had already been initiated in Indochina, and he evidently drew attention to this in the conversation on 6 September. Next day a letter arrived for him from 56, rue Monsieur-le-Prince: 'As a follow-up to our talk yesterday, I send you herewith a copy of the *Revendications* … I take the liberty of asking you to indicate for us what has so far been accomplished regarding our eight demands … because I maintain that they are still unresolved, none of them having yet received a satisfactory solution.'[5]

From this moment onwards Nguyễn Ái Quốc was watched. It was soon clear to the *Sûreté* that he was on close terms with two compatriots who had been known to the police for many years. Phan Văn Trường had come to Paris in 1908, when he was in his early thirties, to study law while teaching Vietnamese. He was now a well-padded barrister and a French citizen, but had not escaped surveillance. Two of his brothers were serving ten-year terms on the prison island of Côn Sơn (Poulo Condore).[6] Phan Chu Trinh, four years older, was a very different character, a scholarly, non-violent but determined nationalist with a wispy beard, briefly prominent as an educational activist in Vietnam. In 1911 he had been deported to Paris; his son, who had perforce accompanied him there, was now dying of tuberculosis.

Trinh, who spoke little French and was penniless, scraped a living as a photographic retoucher while lodging with Trường at 6, Villa des Gobelins, in the 13th *arrondissement*. By late November 1919 the mysterious Nguyễn Ái Quốc was living there too. A frequent visitor was Lam, a *Sûreté* informant known to his employers as 'Jean': he reported heated political arguments that lasted so late into the night that the neighbours complained.

Thanks to Lam, one of the question marks in the police files was erased. He reported that Quốc had not really written the *Revendications* submitted to the Peace Conference: his French was not up to it. What had happened was that he had allowed Trường to use his name. This claim by Lam is often repeated as a plain fact by modern historians. For example, Sophie Quinn-Judge says that 'Phan Van Truong was clearly the author'.[7] But Lam got things wrong and was inconsistent in his reports on Quốc's abilities as a writer of French. Pierre Brocheux makes a more complex story of it: the text was 'drafted by Thanh [i.e. Quốc] with the help of Phan Chu Trinh and written down by Phan Van Truong'.[8] Hue-Tam Ho Tai's formulation is that Nguyen Ai Quac was being used at this stage as a 'collective signature' which Quốc himself eventually personified.[9] It will probably never be known what share each man had in the document.

Lam's reports showed that the trio at the Villa des Gobelins

Phan Chu Trinh (1872–1926) was a civil servant in the Ministry of Rites in Annam (under French protectorate); he submitted a political memorandum in 1908. Sentenced to death, he was reprieved and in 1911 was exiled to Paris at the demand of the Human Rights League. He returned to Indochina in 1925 but died a year later.

Phan Văn Trường (c. 1876–1933) studied law in Paris, then worked as a barrister. Harassed by the police, he was imprisoned from 1914–15. He returned to Indochina in 1924. In 1928, he wrote *Une histoire de conspirateurs annamites à Paris* (1928).

Nguyễn Tất Thành, later **Nguyễn Ái Quốc and Hồ Chí Minh** (1890–1969), worked abroad as a cook etc and lived in Paris 1919–23. He signed the *Revendications* sent to the Paris Peace Conference. He organised resistance based in the Soviet Union and China, and was in Vietnam from 1941. He achieved independence for North Vietnam at the Geneva Conference of 1954, and led the war for unification.

were in touch with various revolutionaries and others on whom the *Sûreté* kept files. Among these was Scie-Ton-Fa, a wealthy Chinese Catholic and a member of the official Chinese delegation to the Peace Conference. They were also on good terms with the Korean Mission in Paris, which was based at 38, rue de Châteaudun and was lobbying for Korea's freedom from Japan; in these discussions both sides recognised that they must tread carefully (Japan, although a colonial power in Korea, had been a source of anti-colonial support to Vietnamese and others under the European yoke). There had also been a recent meeting with Irishman *sieur O'Callaigh*.[10] This was Sean T O'Kelly, future President of Ireland. In 1918, standing for Sinn Fein, he had been elected to the British House of Commons, but he and his colleagues had refused to take their seats and instead set up an Irish parliament in Dublin of which O'Kelly was elected speaker. He had been in Paris since February 1919 and had delivered a demand for Irish independence to the Peace Conference secretariat at the Quai d'Orsay. It achieved nothing.

The Vietnamese appeal to the Peace Conference also failed, and Quốc knew it. Undaunted, he went with Trường's friend Marius Moutet to a Socialist Party meeting critical of the Peace Conference's failures in eastern Asia; he insisted on his right to speak, very much as he would later do at Tours, though as yet he had not the knack of getting the audience on his side. 'His whole time is devoted to politics,' Lam reported. 'He spends his days at the Bibliothèque Nationale, the Bibliothèque Sainte-Geneviève, the Ligue des Droits de l'Homme [Human Rights League] and visiting his unreliable compatriots.'[11] Like Trinh, he earned a little money from photographic work; journalism helped too. One of the first newspaper articles signed Nguyễn Ái Quốc was entitled 'Indochina and Korea: an interesting comparison' and appeared in *Le populaire*; the same byline appeared in the Socialist daily *L'humanité*, more and more regularly as time went on.[12] He was also writing a book, *The Oppressed*, but without the necessary money his best hope of getting it printed was to persuade *L'humanité* to take it on.[13]

The police expert Jean Przyluski, with Lam's help, was meanwhile hard at work. He noted that the mysterious name meant 'Nguyen the Patriot' (Nguyễn is the commonest of all Vietnamese surnames) and that the early spelling Nguyen Ai Quac was evidence of Annamese (central Vietnamese) dialect. Przyluski's colleagues in Hanoi, following up a clue from Paris that the 'real name' might be Nguyễn Tất Thành, discovered that there had been a young man of that name, son of a dismissed Annamese civil servant. Relatives were traced; there was a sister, and she admitted that her brother had a scarred ear. She had heard indirectly that he was in London: yes, an early report alleged that the thin Vietnamese had arrived in Paris from London. Surely further denials would be useless? And so, for the first time, he was summoned on 12 October 1920 to the Préfecture de Police and was interrogated as to his real name. He replied, truthfully, that his name was Nguyễn Ái Quốc. 'Without the slightest doubt we are faced with a false statement,'[14] his interrogator noted angrily. It is a sign of the continuing importance of the thin Vietnamese (henceforth Hồ Chí Minh, or briefly Hồ) that the seven-page police report, summarising progress up to and including this interview, was addressed to Albert Sarraut himself. It told him nothing new.

Gradually Hồ was becoming more certain of the line he must take if his people were to be freed from foreign domination. In Russia, Lenin had declared that 'the liberation of the colonies is possible only together with the liberation of the working class in the imperialist centres … Workers and peasants of Annam, Algeria and Bengal … will gain the possibility of an independent existence only when the workers of Britain and France have toppled Lloyd George and Clemenceau'.[15] Closer at hand, it was the French Socialists who had immediately spoken against the Treaty of Versailles and its 'reduction of entire nations to slavery'.[16] Hồ's own most fruitful contacts had been with these Socialists; their newspaper had become his preferred medium, and its editor a personal friend. At the May Day 1920 Socialist rally at Kremlin-Bicêtre, a brisk walk south from the Villa des Gobelins, he spoke to a cheerful crowd of 2,000 (to whom he was announced as 'secretary of the Vietnamese Socialist Party', imaginary official of an imaginary party). That summer and autumn of 1920 he found fiercest enthusiasm for the anti-colonial cause in the Socialist left wing, among the same people who spoke most strongly in favour of revolutionary Russia and were now proposing to affiliate the French Socialist party with the international communist movement, the Third International or Comintern. And it was Lenin's new and trenchant programme in the *Theses on National and Colonial Questions* (see panel, page 70; published in French translation in *L'humanité* on 16 and 17 July 1920) that turned Hồ into a Leninist and inspired his *L'humanité* article on 'Colonial Policy', published soon afterwards. So, at least, he recalled later in a memoir published in Russian, 'My Path to Leninism'.

By the time Hồ reached Tours in December, his future strategy was becoming clear to him. It was also clear that from the viewpoint of South East Asia the Paris Peace Conference had failed entirely to live up to expectations. Siam alone (the only independent state in the region and an ally of the victorious Entente in the First World War) was invited to send a delegation to the Conference; it was headed by the career diplomat Prince Charoon. And even Siam had nothing to gain from its presence in Paris in 1919 beyond founder membership of the League of Nations and some slight easing of relations with the colonial powers. For the other four territories dealt with in this volume, all the talk of self-determination came to very little. Indochina was at least an unofficial presence at Paris, because (to the dismay of the French authorities) Hồ Chí Minh was on the spot and delivered his *Revendications* to the Conference secretariat, but nothing came of them. In the same year both Burma and the Philippines for the first time sent delegations to their 'imperial' capitals, London and Washington, to press the case for independence. The Burmese mission, led by Ba Pe of the Young Men's Buddhist Association, helped to gain a limited form of self-government. The Philippines already had this, but any further progress that might have been achieved by the Philippine mission, headed by Manuel Quezon, melted away when Woodrow Wilson was succeeded by Warren Harding as American President. Finally, in the Dutch Indies, stirrings during and after 1919 led Henk Sneevliet to represent the territory at the Second Comintern Congress in Moscow. There, following Lenin's lead, he (and soon afterwards Hồ Chí Minh as well) would seek to combine the forces of communism with those of nationalism.

In all five cases, then, the negotiations in Paris in 1919 appear marginal. Yet it was as a direct result of President Wilson's speech to Congress on 8 January 1918 – in which he delivered the Fourteen Points, spoke of freedom and self-determination, and sketched a new political framework for the world – that the question of independence for the peoples of South East Asia was first seriously raised, in South East Asia itself, in Paris and elsewhere. 1919 permanently changed the world.

The young men (most of them were young, all of them happened to be men) who were at the centre of things in that year, when political change began to come to South East Asia, are the focus here. The whole region and all the peoples in it were to be swept by those changes, but this book deals with the five countries already directly affected and with their majority peoples now awakening to world politics. Many drew inspiration from the Japanese victory over Russia in 1905, the first significant defeat of Europeans by Asians in modern times. Many more were stirred to action by the Russian Revolution, the Wilsonian Fourteen Points and the Paris Peace Conference.

The young Hồ Chí Minh. He would achieve independence for North Vietnam in 1954, and lead the war for unification with South Vietnam until his death in 1969.

I
The Lands

1

Sources of East Asian Nationhood

South East Asia as now understood, half continental, half insular, and stretching from the mountainous borders of China and India to the edge of the deep Pacific, is a modern concept, first named, it is said, in South East Asia Command, a strategic union of Allied forces established in 1943 to fight the Japanese. Before that, the islands and coastal states were known collectively as the Indies or East Indies or the Malay Archipelago; the peninsula was Indochina, and its prolongation Malaya. These lands were regarded as part of the Far East or characterised vaguely as Further India.

The new concept was useful and it has taken hold. South East Asia has unity: geographically, with its fertile valleys, abundant water and precipitous, forested mountains; climatically, being subject to the monsoons and the alternation of wet and dry seasons; culturally, with the region's openness to influences from India, China and, more recently, beyond; historically, in a long sequence of powerful states with fluid borders and thriving capital cities; economically, in the balance of local agriculture and valuable water-borne long-distance trade that kept these states prosperous.

Yet South East Asia's diversity in language and culture is as great as is found in any comparable region of the world. For eleven modern nations (Burma or Myanmar, Brunei, Cambodia, Indonesia, Laos, Malaysia, the Philippines, Singapore, Thailand, East Timor and Vietnam), there are eight national languages belonging to four unrelated language families.

Each mainland nation traces its history to a succession of medieval and early modern kingdoms: Burma to the 9th century and the dynasty that built Pagan; Thailand (historically known as Siam) to the ruined capitals of Ayutthaya and its predecessor Sukhothai, founded in the 13th century; Cambodia again to the 9th century and the vast abandoned city of Angkor; Vietnam, with a longer unbroken history than the others, traceable to the 3rd century BC but subject for over a thousand years to Chinese overlordship. In no case is this the full story. Other early kingdoms, speaking different languages and drawing in their own way on Indian influences and on long-distance trade contacts, take the history of each nation and its minority peoples back to the first millennium BC. Further south and in the islands there was again a constellation of kingdoms. The influence of the most powerful of these, Srivijaya, which ruled from central Sumatra in the 7th to 13th centuries, can be traced as far afield as the Philippines to the north-east and Madagascar to the south-west.

China traded with almost the whole region. India's influence was even more pervasive: by way of India came trade, learning, Hinduism, and then Buddhism, and then Islam. No one people, from South East Asia or beyond, ever dominated the region politically. Its very diversity perhaps made that impossible, and China, with its intermittent rule over Vietnam, was the only state from beyond South East Asia to exert any significant power there until, in 1511, the Europeans arrived in force.

Oddly, Afonso de Albuquerque, Governor of the Portuguese

'State of India', had decided to sail west, not east, in that year. A fleet set out under his command from Kochi (Cochin) westwards in the direction of the Red Sea, intending an attack on the Arab traders who were Portugal's chief competitors in the Indian Ocean trade; but he misjudged the monsoon and arrived too late to do anything useful. Rather than be trapped in enemy territory, he returned to base. Something had to be done with the ships that had been gathered at such cost. Eastwards across the Bay of Bengal was the city of Melaka (Malacca), historically a satellite of Srivijaya and a famously busy port commanding the strait that divided Sumatra from the Malay peninsula – the seaway that all vessels plying between India and China must necessarily take. Mahmud Shah, King of Melaka, was rich and independent, ruling extensive territories on both sides of the strait, on close terms with the neighbouring Malay kingdom of Pahang, deferring only to the king of Siam and the emperor of China. And in Melaka there were twenty Portuguese. They had been there, well treated but not allowed to leave, ever since Diogo Lopes de Sequeira had reached Melaka with three ships in 1509 (the first Portuguese ever seen there) and had left hastily after a disagreement with Mahmud Shah, but leaving some of his crew behind. Melaka was so 'majestic in the size of its population, the number of ships in its harbour, and the business transacted between landsmen and seamen', these reluctant visitors reported, that although built in wood it appeared richer than the seaports of India. Its people were Malays. In its harbour were to be found Bengalis, Peguans, Siamese, Javanese, Chinese, Luzonians from the central Philippines, and Ryukyuans from the southernmost Japanese islands.[1] Armed with this information, Albuquerque set out eastwards for Melaka on 20 April 1511. Unproductive negotiations with Mahmud Shah and secret deals with leaders of the Chinese and Javanese trading communities culminated on 24 August in a successful Portuguese assault on the city.

Albuquerque wanted nothing more than a trading base, a stage on the route to the Spice Islands (the Moluccas, not yet visited by any European). Sixty years later Miguel López de Legazpi had an additional motive when, setting out from Mexico, he crossed the Pacific in 93 days and claimed for Philip II of Spain the islands henceforth named the Philippines. Cebu, he reported to his royal patron, was 'so fertile that four days after we took the village the Castilian seeds had already sprouted … We are at the gate and in the vicinity of the most fortunate countries of the world'; he hoped for advantages to God and the Spanish crown 'if this land is settled by Spaniards, as I believe it will be.'[2] If Cebu was good, an exploring party sent out northwards in 1569 discovered that the big island of Luzon was better. 'The land all around this bay, in the part where we anchored, and which the guides declared to be the port of Menilla, was really marvellous … so excellent indications have not been seen in this land, as were seen there.'[3] 'Manilla is now a Spanish city,' a report of 1572 claimed proudly.[4] The Spice Islands were temporarily forgotten; land was the new aim. But Legazpi was far ahead of his time, and even in the Philippines very little European settlement actually took place.

Through the 17th and 18th centuries these islands – gradually brought under Spanish administration, not without opposition – remained the only sizeable colonial possession in the whole of South East Asia. Elsewhere Europeans were content to fight one another and local rulers for spice monopolies and other trading rights, acquiring a minimum of territory in the process. Among the islands of the archipelago, and along the mainland coast, Portuguese footholds gave way in turn to Spanish, Dutch and British. Batavia (Jakarta), the centre of Dutch power in the East Indies, was the most impressive of these, but at first very little land was ruled directly from it. Then, in the late 1700s, largely owing to competition from the Caribbean, the monopolies were broken; the cloves and nutmeg of the Spice Islands, the pepper, camphor and cinnamon produced elsewhere in the region, ceased to command a high price. The focus of European interest shifted to the trade with China.

Religion had thus far remained a separate impulse. Christianity spread in the Philippines with the backing of the Spanish administration; in other countries – notably in Vietnam, where French Catholics had a long-established presence – the missionaries worked well beyond the reach of European support, until in 1787 French volunteers, at missionary request, fought successfully to re-establish the Nguyễn dynasty in Vietnam, thus ending a long period of civil strife.

Around 1800, then, Spain controlled the Philippines without serious opposition. The East Indies, scene of continuing disputes between Britain and the Netherlands, largely consisted of small kingdoms and tribal territories over which Dutch power, direct and indirect, was spreading. On the mainland, Burma had reached roughly its present extent after its ruling dynasty conquered Pegu, Tenasserim and Arakan; Amarapura had recently supplanted Ava as Burmese capital city. Newly-reunited Vietnam was not unlike the modern state in size and shape; in 1802 the capital was to be established at Huế. But Siam, with its newly-built capital Krungthep Mahanakhon (Bangkok), was much more extensive than modern Thailand. Its borderlands, largely controlled indirectly through subordinate princes, extended southwards deep into the Malay peninsula, and northeastwards across the whole of Laos, which consisted of three principalities subject to Siamese overlordship. Cambodia, all-powerful in the past, was now a subject state, sometimes acknowledging the suzerainty of Vietnam, but around 1800 firmly controlled by Siam.

The new imperialism (if that is what it was) of the 19th century, the competition by European powers for territory in South East Asia, had no single impulse. In hindsight two catalysts within the region can be recognised. The first was the French intervention in Vietnam in 1787, which resulted in no immediate acquisition of land but set up the conditions for France's attack on Cochinchine in 1858 (ostensibly in support of missionaries), leading to annexation in 1862 followed by steady expansion northwards. The second catalyst was the Anglo-Dutch Treaty of 1824, in which the Straits of Malacca were accepted by both sides as the boundary of their respective spheres of influence. From this date onwards the Netherlands were able to extend their power and commerce without competition in what by 1900 had in truth become the Dutch Indies. The British, with their new base at Singapore, could spread their influence and trading networks unchallenged among the Malay states of the peninsula; from their established position in India they were free to pursue without opposition the economic domination, and eventually annexation, of Burma. In turn, neither the Dutch nor the British challenged France for influence in Vietnam and its hinterland.

In 1885, the year in which Britain put an end to Burma's independence, a journalist and future administrator, J G Scott, explained matters thus: 'The entire country ... lay in our power, and we might have annexed the whole of it in 1852. We gave back the Upper Provinces ... on the distinct understanding that good order and a good government were to be maintained, and that no molestation was to be offered to us.' Good government was not maintained in royal Burma, he continued, and

There were three stages in Britain's annexation of Burma. In the First Anglo-Burmese War, 1824–6, the British Empire gained three provinces: Assam and Arakan, adjacent to British India, and also Tenasserim in Burma's far south. Tenasserim, closer to Malaya than to India, was at first governed as an appendage of Britain's Malay possessions.

The Second War, 1852–3, resulted in the division of Burma's heartland: 'Upper Burma', the inland region, remained independent but with no access to the sea. The coastal districts were annexed by Britain; Rangoon (Yangon), previously insignificant, soon became the capital of British Burma, a province of the Indian Empire.

The Third War opened in 1885. In a sense it ended in weeks, with the surrender of the Burmese army, the occupation of Mandalay and King Thibaw's departure into exile; but 'pacification' and the gradual annexation of tributary states continued into the 1890s.

British Burma was governed by a Chief Commissioner, then a Lieutenant-Governor, then (from 1923) a Governor. Until 1937 these answered to the Government of India and the India Office, and thereafter to the Colonial Office.

British traders were molested; and, after all, 'the two Burmas are really but one country with no natural divisions'.[5]

'The Mandalay campaign was undertaken with a light heart,' a colleague wrote soon afterwards, 'in the belief that the people of Upper Burma would welcome us with open arms. Events have proved how ill-founded the belief was ... the people do not want us any more than they did thirty years ago [and] are still carrying on a guerilla warfare against us.'[6] There was similar opposition to French expansion in Vietnam, desultory and eventually unsuccessful but persistent and disruptive. The Dutch faced fiercer opposition in parts of the Indies, notably in northern Sumatra where they took on the powerful Muslim state of Aceh. The new conquests brought economic development, but they also brought a cash economy, poverty, bankruptcy, unemployment and social disruption. Resentment rose, not only against the Europeans, but even more against Indian

> **THE KINGS OF SIAM**
> Chulalongkorn or Rama V (1853–1910), son of King Mongkut by his niece Debsirindra, succeeded in 1868. He ceded territory to France and Britain but kept Siam independent. When he died in 1910, he was succeeded by the eldest of his sons by Saowabha, his sister and favourite wife –
> Vajiravudh or Rama VI (1881–1925) studied at Sandhurst and Oxford. Founder of the Wild Tigers, proponent of Thai nationalism and of participation in the First World War, he encouraged treaty renegotiations at the Paris Peace Conference and elsewhere. With no sons, he was succeeded by his only surviving full brother –
> Prajadhipok or Rama VII (1893–1941), an Old Etonian, who undertook military studies in Britain and France. He proclaimed constitutional monarchy in 1932, but abdicated three years later, in 1935, in favour of his nephew Ananda Mahidol. He retired to Cranleigh in south-east England, and died at nearby Virginia Water.

and Chinese migrants who came as labourers, traders and settlers and eventually formed large and prosperous minorities. This 'double colonialism', as Rabindranath Tagore observed it in Burma,[7] existed throughout South East Asia. Very little new wealth reached the indigenous population.

And so, by 1900, all significant South East Asian countries had fallen to the Europeans with the single exception of Siam; even Siam was anything but secure, having given half its borderlands to France and Britain in the struggle to maintain independence. However, unlike the last kings of Burma, Siam's Chakri dynasty was alive to the need for change. During the long reign of Chulalongkorn there were scholarships for young Siamese to attend European schools and universities. Foreign advisers became a familiar sight in Government ministries. Friendships were cultivated with the Russian and British royal families.

Everywhere (except at first in Siam) those who observed the new foreign-led prosperity and had no share in it were natural recruits for the resistance movements of the 20th century, insignificant and unorganised as such movements were at first. Colonial administrations found the idea of resistance difficult to grasp. Were they not introducing peace, prosperity, opportunity, education? Surely no civilisable person would resist? The conceptual problem is evident both from the barbarous punishments meted out to those who did resist, albeit peacefully, and from the comfortingly pejorative terms that all administrations adopted for those who were prepared to take this disruption as far as violence. In the Philippines these were 'bandits'; in Burma they were 'dacoits'; in Indochina they were 'pirates'. They were beyond civilisation, and by definition deserved the summary trials, imprisonments for life, deportations and public executions that all administrations practised.

In the first such resistance movement, in 1896 the Philippines rose up against the weakening power of Spain. It seemed momentarily that with help from the United States, destined for victory in the Spanish-American War, the Philippines would actually gain independence. A draft announcement was prepared for the Hongkong Junta, the exile organisation over which the Filipino leader Emilio Aguinaldo presided: 'Divine Providence is about to place independence within our reach ... The Americans, not from mercenary motives but for the sake of humanity ... will find means to assist us. They are our redeemers!' [8] The Americans eventually decided otherwise when control of the Philippines passed to them under the Treaty of Paris. Filipino forces boldly took on the United States, until Aguinaldo,

> 'Divine Providence is about to place independence within our reach. The Americans will find means to assist us. They are our redeemers!'
>
> **PROCLAMATION PREPARED FOR THE PHILIPPINE RESISTANCE, 16 MAY 1898**

captured on 23 March 1901, advised his followers to surrender. Remaining resistance was ruthlessly crushed.

A difficulty for any resistance movement was that the Europeans had won so comprehensively. Then in 1905 came rumours of war between Japan and Russia, and shortly afterwards the astonishing, invigorating news of Japan's victory, evidence for a proposition that many would until then have dismissed as fantasy. It was possible for an Asian and a European power to fight a war and for the Europeans to be defeated.

U Chit Hlaing in a photographic portrait by Bassano in November 1931.

II

The Lives: The Struggle for Self-Determination

2
The Voice of Young Burma, 1906–22

One morning, early in 1906, three young men walked east along Dalhousie Street in central Rangoon (Yangon). It was pleasantly cool, the sun still low in the sky, the crowded, modern, colonial city hardly awake. About to cross Judah Ezekiel Street, they paused and glanced towards the YMCA hostel on the opposite corner. 'A Young Men's Buddhist Association,' said one. It might have been Ba Pe, 23, a country boy studying at Government College and about to gain his BA (Calcutta, external); unable to afford to study abroad he would instead take a teaching post at St Paul's High School. It might have been Maung Gyi, a future Education Minister; it might have been their friend Hla Pe, who was to start a short-lived weekly paper, *The Burman*, in 1909. It does not matter who said it, because all three agreed. They would set up a Young Men's Buddhist Association (YMBA). No need for hostels; the innocuous name would allow them, under Government eyes, to meet, to talk and, naturally, to talk politics.[1] With hindsight, the beginnings of modern Burmese nationalism can be dated to this moment: eighty years after the British had invaded Lower Burma, twenty years since their rapid conquest of Upper Burma and fifteen years since, in their view, 'pacification' was substantially complete.

Or else, with John Furnivall, we may locate 'the dawn of nationalism in Burma' to a certain YMBA meeting in early August 1908. Furnivall, then a young officer in the Indian Civil Service, attended because he had known the speaker, May Oung, before May Oung left to study law in London, and because the topic, 'The Young Burman: his life and notions', amused him. He immediately recognised it as a play on the title of a classic ethnographic text, J G Scott's *The Burman: his life and notions.*

'Young' was the new and significant word. May Oung spoke of those Burmans, like himself, who had 'the not unmixed blessing of a Western education … It was on them and those like them – on their training, acquirements, exertions – that the future of their race would in no small measure depend.' What followed might have made his old acquaintance Furnivall uncomfortable. 'On all sides [May Oung warned his audience] they saw the ceaseless, ebbless tide of foreign civilisation and learning steadily creeping over the land, and it seemed to him that unless they prepared themselves to meet it, to overcome it, and to apply it to their own needs … their very existence as a distinct nationality would be swept away, submerged, irretrievably lost.'[2] He foresaw rapid social decay and the loss of respect for Buddhism and traditional values. Burma was becoming economically dependent on the Empire.

Ba Pe (1883–?) was joint founder and leader of the Young Men's Buddhist Association and founding editor of *Thuriya*. He was a member of the 1919 and 1920 London delegations; Education Minister; head of the Burmese Chamber of Commerce; and Home Minister. Gaoled in 1941, he probably died in prison.

May Oung (1880–1926) studied law in London. He was joint founder of the Burma Research Society, 1910 and Home Minister 1924–6.

As his own membership demonstrates, the YMBA had by then begun to attract not only penniless young intellectuals but also rising barristers and professional men, few in number but none the less influential. Two years later May Oung and Furnivall co-founded the Burma Research Society, in which for three-quarters of a century Burmese and Britons would join to study and record Burmese culture. At the same time, and more important to the spread of nationalism, came the growth of a Burmese press, beginning with the long-running *Thuriya* ('*The Sun*'), founded in 1911, edited jointly during those early years by Ba Pe and Hla Pe. It was naturally sympathetic to the YMBA, and carried regular satirical comment by the playwright Saya Lun (reprinted in 1914 under the half-scriptural title *Bo htika,* 'Commentary on Masters'). Crucial, though, was the rapid spread of YMBAs through the cities and towns of Burma. Already in 1910, when the first national meeting was held, there were twenty-two affiliated associations. During these early years all meetings voted loyalty to the Crown and gratitude for the favour of British administration, but gradually political opinions began to be expressed publicly. The 1915 All Burma Conference submitted several 'memorials' (that is, written recommendations) to Government on educational and religious matters; the appointment of a Minister of Buddhist Affairs was suggested.

In the First World War Burma was not called on to supply troops; for better or worse the Burmese army had been left to melt away in 1885 and had never been reconstituted. The territory's economic dependence on the Empire and its increasing social fragility were to be painfully demonstrated. In rural Lower Burma, ever more beset by indebtedness to Indian and other colonial landlords, there had perforce been a massive increase in the growing of rice, the best available cash crop for export. Suddenly there were no ships to export the rice: total capacity was reduced by submarine warfare and remaining vessels were commandeered to carry soldiers and supplies for the war in Europe. The rice price collapsed just as land taxes increased steeply, leading to bankruptcies and expropriation. Migration into the cities and to Upper Burma brought social disruption and crime. The British district commissioner of Akyab, in a report to superiors, unknowingly supported May Oung's diagnosis: the 'reënforcement [*sic*] of the social instincts which every society has devised … are … custom, religion, and criminal law. The Government of Burma has relied almost entirely on the last named, and it is to the decay of the first two that I would attribute the present tendencies to crime.'[3]

Against this background, events in 1917 and 1918 displayed the inelasticity of the British administration and the readiness of the YMBAs and others to take the initiative. Harcourt Butler, Lieutenant-Governor of Burma since 1915, was an enthusiast for education but also for the 'Imperial Idea', which could be inculcated in Burma, he thought, by propaganda, chiefly in schools and colleges. These must therefore be run by Britons, not by American missionaries or Buddhist abbots.[4] His long-winded schemes for songs, textbooks, public meetings and school lessons on the benefits of Empire met with no enthusiasm; it is unsurprising that objections were raised at the fifth All Burma Conference in October 1917. By that time, however, Butler's term as Lieutenant-Governor was over; Burma's 'Imperial Idea' died with him, and the Conference gave more attention to a recently-reported statement in the House of Commons on 20 August 1917 by Edwin Montagu, the Liberal Secretary of State for India newly-appointed in Lloyd George's cabinet. He had announced that India would move towards 'the progressive realization of responsible self-government …

as an integral part of the British Empire'.[5] Burma, it was under-stood, would be a mere province of this self-governing India; Montagu (alongside Lord Chelmsford, the current Viceroy of India) was to tour India, but not Burma, to gather opinions before final legislation.

In Rangoon, heated public meetings to discuss this unsat-isfactory prospect led to a decisive step by the YMBA Confer-ence: it would pay for a four-man delegation to go to Calcutta to address Montagu and Chelmsford. Ba Pe, widely known as an editor and still a prominent radical in the association, was to be its spokesman. It presented a 'memorial' that proposed replacing the present Legislative Council (which was wholly Governor-appointed and had a permanent British majority) with a new, largely elected body of 75 members; reporting to this would be a cabinet of six. But competing delegations at Calcutta formed a discordant chorus, among them a group of pliant conservatives, their fares paid by the British Burma administration (alerted by advance reading of the YMBA memorial). The Buddhist establishment of Mandalay sent a mission; so did the Karen people of the south-eastern hills, largely Christian, quite out of sympathy with Rangoon opinion and unwilling to be swamped in a Burman tide. The Karen del-egate San C Po stated flatly that 'the country is not yet in a fit state for self-government. Burma is inhabited by many differ-ent races, differing in states of civilisation, differing in religion and social development; hence Burma will have still to undergo many years of strenuous training under British governance … it is in a state of transition still, and as yet the benefits of free government are not quite fully appreciated'.[6]

Even so, it is a shock to read Montagu's private estimate of the Burmese: 'Nice simple-minded people with beautiful clothes. Complete loyalty; no sign of political unrest.'[7] Possibly, in his verbal evidence, Ba Pe gave too much time to urging the need for a university (which was accepted) and his insistence that Burma was separate from India. Possibly he was too polite – though less polite than May Oung, the London-educated barrister, would have been if he had led the team as was originally intended. One month before the departure for India, *Thuriya* had published a cartoon depicting a British couple riding on the back of a venerable pagoda trustee and thanking him for letting them visit the Shwedagon pagoda without taking off their shoes. All who saw it knew three things: one took off one's shoes before entering a temple; Europeans excepted themselves from the rule; and no one dared to insist. Police Commissioner E C S Shuttleworth (famous only for this act and for his studies of Indian prostitution) called in Ba Pe and his fellow editors for a dressing-down. Refusing to apologise, they called a public YMBA meeting in early November 1917, at which the all-too-moderate May Oung, unable to silence the radicals, resigned his membership and led a walkout. The chair on this occasion was taken and the subsequent nationwide campaign was triumphantly led by his younger contemporary, a provincial lawyer from Prome, Thein Maung. Henceforth Burmese temples were visited with shoes removed – or, by members of the colonial establishment, not at all.[8] The moderates had been ousted. A line had been drawn around the British. It was a famous victory.

By the time the Montagu-Chelmsford Report was published in late summer 1918, much more might have been said about Burma than it attempted. 'The desire for elective institutions has not developed in Burma': this leaned heavily on Karen opinion. 'Burma is not India': here, certainly, all agreed. 'Its people belong to another stage of political development, and its problems are altogether different.'[9] There was an admixture of truth in this, but it led to a weak conclusion: reform in

India should begin at once, but in Burma nothing should be done quickly. Butler's successor Reginald Craddock, the new Lieutenant-Governor, was instructed to prepare a scheme for adapting the proposed India reforms to Burma.

Born in Dharamsala, the old headquarters of the British Indian Empire, just a year after the Viceroy Lord Elgin died there, Craddock had acquired from long service in India a hearty dislike for political agitation. His reading had told him that there was none in Burma. Throughout his term of office his official reports either attributed political disturbances to Indian infiltrators or left them unmentioned. Burmans were 'content to pursue their private callings and leave affairs of State alone, secure in the sincerity and impartiality of their British officers', he wrote in an annual report.[10] Such claims apparently went unquestioned in London; there was always more happening in Burma than London cared to ask about.

'The desire for elective institutions has not developed in Burma.'

MONTAGU–CHELMSFORD REPORT, 1918

The Habitual Offenders Act 1918 and the notorious Rowlatt Act (the same that occasioned Gandhi's non-cooperation movement) allowed the police to arrest political offenders on suspicion and to restrict suspected troublemakers to distant locations. The even more drastic powers of the so-called Criminal Tribes Act, as revised in India in 1911, were put to effective use. Membership of the YMBAs, once encouraged, was now forbidden to Government employees, and a close police watch was kept on its officials and its meetings.

At the war's end in November 1918, the victorious powers set to work on the Peace. At the Paris Peace Conference India was represented within the British delegation. Needless to say, issues of self-government never surfaced. Burma, one of

THE ROWLATT ACT

In 1918, the Viceroy of India, Viscount Chelmsford, set up a committee to investigate 'criminal conspiracies connected with the revolutionary movement in India' and its suspected links with Germany and Russia. The result was legislation that is often briefly named after the British judge who chaired the committee, Sir Sidney Rowlatt. The Anarchical and Revolutionary Crimes Act, or 'Rowlatt Act', limited to three years from March 1919, empowered the Government of India to use imprisonment without trial and press censorship to suppress political agitation and sedition. In effect, this 1919 measure prolonged into peacetime the temporary restrictions imposed during the First World War by the Defence of India Act 1915, aimed against seditious acts in favour of Britain's enemies. It was complemented by two others. The Habitual Offenders Act of 1918 allowed so-called 'habitual offenders' to be restricted to a certain district and required to report regularly to the police (thus, in effect, exiled); the Criminal Tribes Act (1871; amended in 1911 and again in 1924) allowed similar restrictions to be imposed on whole communities said to be addicted to criminal activity. Politicians in London were well aware of the effect in India of these restrictions; the fact that they also applied to Burma was scarcely noticed.

the largest territories for which the British Government of India was responsible, went unmentioned. In Burma, meanwhile, political trouble threatened on two fronts. Craddock's draft reform scheme, submitted to the Government of India at Simla, in December 1918, had proposed an electoral roll of taxpayers (a small minority) to elect local councils: these would in turn elect 52 of the 75 members of a 'legislative' council – whose recommendations, however, could in nearly every case be overruled by the Governor.

The backward thrust of the scheme aroused intense dissatisfaction in Burma; its complexity was as if calculated to exclude Burmese from all but the most local level of government. A vigorous press campaign was soon under way. Meanwhile a committee of two Burmese and twelve Britons, led by Mark Hunter, a former schoolmaster and close associate of Craddock newly arrived from India as Director of Public Instruction, proposed a new basis for university education in Burma. The University Bill that was circulated at the end of 1918 leaned heavily on the British educational system in syllabuses and course structure, overlooking Burmese history and culture entirely. Another glaring fault was that it would lengthen higher education and channel it wholly into a well-controlled and expensive residential university in Rangoon. On this system even such as Ba Pe could not have afforded to complete a degree, and there were many deserving students whose families were poorer than his.

At this critical moment two very different figures, equally charismatic, entered the scene. The Buddhist monk Ottama was already known in his native Burma for occasional writings in *Thuriya* and for a book on Japan published in 1914; he was known in India too as member both of the secular Indian National Congress and the religious-based nationalist organisation Hindu Mahasabha. He now reappeared in Burma after many years of study, teaching and politics abroad during which he forged links between Buddhist Japan, the nationalist thinkers of Bengal and the growing nationalism of Burma. The name he adopted, Ottama, was highly significant: it was borrowed from a monastic predecessor who, in the stirring tradition of Bankim Chandra Chattopadhyay's Bengali novel *Anandamath* (1882), had thrown off his robe to fight the British invaders of Upper Burma, with no little success. He was captured and hanged as a dacoit in 1889, and his fame endured among both Burmans and British. Now, in 1919, the new Ottama – who remained a monk and never bore arms – wrote and spoke forcefully against the British administration. He saw and urged the need for an alliance between the nationalist movement and the monks, a powerful and as yet untapped force in this deeply religious culture in which most men spent several youthful years in monastic garb. A related cause, an idea that grew from his experience in Japan and Bengal, was that of a national Buddhist college.

The other political newcomer, a wealthy, London-educated Burman teak merchant and generous benefactor of Buddhist education, Chit Hlaing, had first come to national notice in late 1918 when the Sixth YMBA All Burma Conference was held in his home city of Moulmein and he was invited to preside. Unlike the earlier succession of more-or-less annual YMBA presidents (Ba Pe had been one of them) Chit Hlaing determined to retain the role; his adaptability to events and well-directed munificence were to ensure a rapidly-growing personal following. It was Chit Hlaing who made the first public response to the proposed University Bill, in a memorandum to the Governor, dated 28 January 1919, which stressed the high cost imposed on potential students and their families by residential study. He urged that wider provision must be made by allowing other institutions, Buddhist, Christian or secular, to affiliate to the university. These comments were reprinted in full in the Burmese press. Almost immediately Ba Pe, with Thein Maung and others, submitted a second comment on the university project. They urged shortening the term of study, which seemed likely to extend to five years in many cases; they urged increasing the proposed student numbers and adding study of Burmese history and literature. This memorandum, too, was reprinted in the press, but Chit Hlaing's had attracted more attention, and he was still in the public eye at the moment when the YMBAs, now more than 200 in number with a total membership of 10,000, at last decided to turn their annual conference into a permanent national body. The first steps of the new General Council of Young Men's Buddhist and Allied Associations were taken – Chit Hlaing presiding – on 18 May

1919. It would send a delegation to London to oppose Craddock's reform scheme and demand partial autonomy on the same terms that the Montagu-Chelmsford Report had proposed for India (dyarchy: under which security and finance would remain under British control). It was probably with Chit Hlaing's personal help that the necessary funding of £2,000 for the London delegation was found.

Informed of this prospect,[11] Craddock now sent a revised scheme to the Government of India at Simla. It contained several changes of detail, but none of substance, and the delegation found no reason to delay its journey. The satirical verve of Saya Lun was an assurance of Burma's support for its emissaries; his *Thuriya* columns of this period were to be collected under the title *Daung htika* ('Commentary on Peacocks'). The peacock was a symbol of the lost Burmese monarchy. The delegates were already in touch with a sympathiser in London, Bernard Houghton, a considerable linguistic scholar who before his retirement from the Burma administration had been Commissioner of Pegu. He had recently written to the *Burma Observer* making the point that in current circumstances the once-popular argument 'Burma is not India' should be quietly dropped: it was a gift to an administration wishing to refuse political advance in Burma. Thus on 7 July 1919, just as the Paris Peace Conference was drawing to its close, the YMBA delegates sailed from

U Ottama (*c.* 1880–1939) was a Buddhist scholar who studied in Japan and India; from 1919 he spoke and wrote against colonialism in Burma. He continued to travel until at least 1935 but was frequently arrested. He died in hospital in Rangoon in 1939.

Chit Hlaing (1879–1952), was born in Moulmein. He studied law in London, then entered the family business as a teak merchant. The free-spending president of YMBA/GCBA from 1919, he was politically prominent during the 1920s. He was imprisoned on the Prince of Wales's visit to Burma in 1921, but was invited to George VI's coronation in 1937.

Rangoon bound for London, where they would demand partial autonomy for Burma on terms analogous to those already projected for India. The three were U Pu (a future Prime Minister) from the moderate Burma Reform League; Tun Shein, headmaster of the Buddhist School at Mandalay, chosen to represent the religious establishment; and Ba Pe, now at 36 a father-figure of the Young Men's Buddhist Association which, thirteen years ago in Dalhousie Street, he had helped to found. The ever-growing and ever more political organisation had come to dominate his life.

The delegation reached London on 8 August. On that very day, back in Burma, Craddock in a gubernatorial speech pointedly referred to 'Young Burma' and its London delegation. Taking the hint offered by Houghton's article, he aimed to stir his audience's suspicions. Thus far, he said, he had 'made strong representations in high quarters' that Burma 'did not want to be absorbed in India, but if "Young Burma" represented the voice of the people he must revise his strong recommendations'. In effect, he threatened to recommend that Burma should be absorbed into India. This produced an immediate response quite contrary to his intention: a mass meeting in Rangoon, not only filling but overflowing Jubilee Hall, at which, under Chit Hlaing's chairmanship, it was hastily agreed that Burma must be included in the India reforms if the alternative was no reform at all.

At breakfast on 14 August the London delegates were reminded uncomfortably of home. The Times carried a report of Craddock's speech under the curious headline 'Paid emissaries in Burma'. This sparked a riposte by Houghton ('you might as well talk of the speakers and agents of the Conservative or Liberal parties in England as paid emissaries')[12] and further letters from old Burma hands; but The Times was not

Craddock's only channel of communication. In September, noting that the YMBA had just held a joint meeting with the Muslim League and the Burma branch of the Indian National Congress, he wrote to Lord Chelmsford, urging the convenient opinion that 'a demand for reforms on the Indian model has not been a spontaneous or indigenous growth in Burma'.[13] Soon afterwards, in a letter that was copied to Montagu, he threw doubt on the loyalty of headmaster Tun Shein, one of the London delegates. Tun Shein, he said, had been 'teaching politics in the school against the wishes of the managers' and had made available to pupils newspapers like the *Burma Observer*, of which 'every issue … contained an attack upon Government'.[14]

In London, U Pu was invited to address the parliamentary Joint Select Committee then at work on the India reforms, but that was all: no dialogue was allowed. Although there is little record of any formal proceedings, we can observe the delegation's success in contacts with the press; Ba Pe's journalistic experience helped here. By November *The Times*, formerly unsympathetic, had come round to the view that 'the treatment of Burma is at present the one great flaw in the Bill … Burma's isolation should not be permitted to continue'.[15] We can also observe the impressive results of the contacts that Houghton was able to arrange with MPs. Montagu gave verbal assurances that Burma should have a constitution analogous to India's, perhaps a year later, and that Burmese opinion would be consulted before legislation; Burma would at all events become a 'Governor's province', separate from and administratively equal with India. As Craddock later viewed it, Montagu 'had begun to queer the pitch' for his scheme. 'I know what the Burmans cabled and wrote concerning the statements alleged to have been made to them by Mr Montagu. These statements were such as to encourage the agitation and induce them to demand a scheme at least as advanced as that given to India.'[16]

In the early weeks of 1920 the three delegates returned to Rangoon, heroes of the hour. In their absence Craddock had gone as far as to press for Tun Shein's dismissal from his headmastership. The matter was raised in the House of Commons, where Montagu was asked to take 'necessary steps to secure that British subjects in Burma are not penalised for giving expression to their legitimate political convictions';[17] it was perhaps never resolved because, almost immediately on his return, Tun Shein died.

The delegates had been greeted by three unwelcome items of news. The Karens, who opposed change, were now separately represented in London. The Craddock scheme was not dead after all; Craddock was about to travel to Simla, headquarters of British India, to put the finishing touches to it. Worst of all, what the delegation had achieved was no longer what the General Council wanted: there must now be reform on terms equal with those offered to India and on the same timetable. Ba Pe and U Pu resigned themselves to return to London. This time the third delegate would be 'Shoe' Thein Maung. On 10 April, just as they were leaving Rangoon, Craddock's finished scheme was circulated. In essence it was unchanged; it hinted at the undesirability of political strife, 'so foreign to the nature of the people, and so inimical to their true interests'.[18]

The second London mission – which dragged on from May 1920 to January 1921 – began ominously. In June the Craddock scheme was published as a parliamentary White Paper. Craddock's Chief Secretary had meanwhile taken the opportunity to question confidentially the soundness both of the delegation, 'representative of a small and limited … class of intellectuals', and of its unofficial adviser Bernard Houghton, 'always known to hold advanced views'.[19] And the Karen case against reform had gained some publicity. All this signified little. Houghton again set up contacts, notably with Labour sympathisers. No one liked the Craddock scheme, and the House of Commons was duly apprised of its faults. Montagu had already promised Burmese reforms analogous to India's, the Joint Select Committee had confirmed the promise, and the delegation now presented him with a petition asking for its fulfilment. The only problem was that no detailed scheme existed different from but analogous to the Indian one; this was precisely what Craddock had failed to provide. Finally, on 13 December, a statement by Montagu promised a short Bill in the next session of Parliament, applying dyarchy on the Indian pattern to Burma. It was the quickest way out.

The delegation returned to a changed political scene. The body they represented had transformed itself once more: at the eighth All Burma Conference, at Prome in October 1920, it had become the General Council of Burmese Associations (GCBA), and Chit Hlaing, his popularity still increasing, was leading it further into radicalism, with endless political resolutions both critical and constructive. Among other issues emerged once again the administration's undermining of organised Buddhism: the Conference called for the restoration of the religious supremacy of Mandalay to monasteries in Lower Burma, interdicted ever since the British takeover in 1852. Nothing was done; hence it scarcely mattered that the charismatic Ottama, now travelling Burma and speaking to massive crowds, had failed to charm the Buddhist establishment. It had no authority in any case. All that counted was that he filled politically-minded young monks and young Buddhists in general with eagerness. He preached the defence of Burmese religion and culture from the invader. His preferred methods, like Gandhi's non-cooperation tactics in India, were peaceful but uncompromising. 'Craddock Go Home', he dared to write in *Thuriya*, and neither he nor the newspaper was punished for it. The goal for his followers, and (by default) for the Association as well, had moved far beyond dyarchy in the direction of 'home rule', Dominion status, or independence.

The single issue that polarised opinion was that of the University of Rangoon, which was to unite Rangoon College and the American missionaries' Judson College. Its 24-member Senate would include just two Burmese and its 56-man Council five Burmese. Demands to increase these numbers, to allow other colleges to affiliate, or (failing all else) to postpone legislation until Burma had its promised dyarchy, were outvoted or overruled. Suggested amendments having been blithely dismissed, the administration's University Bill became law on 1 December,[20] the last possible moment, since the University was to be formally inaugurated on 7 December. Almost unanimously (if the evidence can be counted reliable) politically-conscious Burma had wanted a university, but not *this* university.

On 4 December 600 students from both colleges met at Shwegyin monastery (at Bahan on the northern edge of Rangoon) for what had been announced as an inter-college debate. They decided on a 'boycott', a walk-out, to take place at the moment Reginald Craddock began his inauguration address. Their plan leaked out, so to keep the initiative the students turned their boycott into an indefinite strike, beginning immediately. Vacating their dormitories, they found the Shwegyin monks and novices ready to share sleeping space. The planned inauguration was hastily cancelled.

'We intend to smash the University Act, which is but an instrument forged by the government to keep the nation in chains.'

UNIVERSITY BOYCOTT COMMITTEE, 1920

The strike was potentially divisive. Karen and 'Anglo-Indian' students opposed it; even *Thuriya* at first urged an end to it; the authorities threatened suspensions and expulsions. But a strong current of opinion was with the strikers, who announced: 'We intend to smash the University Act, which is but an instrument forged by the government to keep the nation in chains … Nothing can save the nation but a proud and indomitable stand on the part of Young Burma.' [21]

Schoolchildren and college students across Burma followed suit; charitable Buddhists and local YMBA branches supported them; Burmese schoolteachers, a hitherto silent majority, met and demanded changes of their own.

'A substratum of reason was discoverable in the position taken up by these students.'

THE TIMES, 24 MAY 1921

Boycott, *boingkauk*, was henceforth a Burmese word, immortalised in the title of Saya Lun's satirical *Boingkauk htika* 'Commentary on Boycotts'. Some 'mischief-makers' were arrested by a misapplication of the Defence of India Act. This evidently aroused unease in India and Britain, as a result of which an ineffective Anti-Boycott Act, specific to Burma, was eventually imposed.[22] Five months after the boycott began, even *The Times* belatedly noticed it: 'Suddenly, without warning the college students went on strike … their ring-leaders were … those who had little chance of passing any examination … these constituted no small proportion of the total', though it conceded that 'a substratum of reason was discoverable in the position taken up by these students'. Those 'ringleaders', incidentally, included two future headmasters, a future ambassador and two future cabinet ministers.[23]

To fill the educational vacuum 'national schools', an embryonic alternative education system rooted in Burma's Buddhist culture, began to appear, often in monasteries. Ottama had certainly helped to inspire this movement, and many of the striking students temporarily volunteered as teachers in the new impromptu schools. In January the GCBA set up a National Education Committee. It was chaired by Maung Gyi, and Ba Pe was a member; meanwhile Hla Pe, currently a Burman appointee on the Legislative Council, attempted to put the student case there. All three of the 1906 YMBA founders were once again at the centre of events. By contrast May Oung, speaker at the historic meeting in 1908, was now identified with loyalism. He also had been appointed to the Legislative Council; alone among Burman members he had voted in favour of the University Bill.

In 1921, for the first time, the administration annual report mentions political dissent, though with the customary implication that it was alien to the Burmese character: there had been 'a rapid development of political activity among the people which few, if any, of those most conversant with the psychology of the people ever predicted, or could have predicted'.[24] In July, after about two years of fervent political speaking and writing during which his popularity had grown continually, Ottama was arrested for sedition (the arrest led to rioting) and was sentenced to ten months' imprisonment. One month later the national schools movement reached a kind of climax with the foundation of a National College, aiming at independent, non-British university-level teaching, at the hospitable Shwegyin monastery; Ottama had urged just such a foundation on his reappearance in Burma in 1919. Using volunteer teachers, and no Britons, the college drew heavily on Bengali academic expertise, but U Pu was college president and the satirist and poet Saya Lun became Professor of Burmese.[25]

In London Montagu kept his promise. It was formally confirmed on 7 October 1921 that Burma, now regarded as 'analogous to India', would get dyarchy; a committee chaired by Sir Frederick Whyte (currently president of India's Legislative Assembly) would immediately visit Burma to gather local opinion, and Burma's principal demands would be met. So it was no failure on Montagu's part that led to the resulting impasse; it was rather that opinion in Burma had moved too fast for London. At the end of October the GCBA held its biggest All Burma Conference ever, with claimed attendance as high as 30,000. With Ottama out of circulation, its president Chit Hlaing had no rival for national adulation, and everywhere he went he was shaded by two golden umbrellas. The conference's big decisions, consequences of the general policy of non-cooperation and predictable responses to the Anti-Boycott Act, were to boycott both the Whyte committee and the impending visit by the Prince of Wales (the future King Edward VIII). Would the Legislative Council elections also be boycotted? That fiercely-contested decision was referred to a committee headed by Ba Pe.

'Whyte go back!' the banners read. The Whyte committee did its best in spite of the boycott. The evidence offered by two who decided not to stay away – May Oung and his long-standing friend John Furnivall – figures prominently in its report, alongside that of San C Po who represented the Karens. All three believed that the advance towards self-government was too fast and ill-prepared.

People had begun speaking of Chit Hlaing as the 'uncrowned king of Burma'. With the Prince's visit imminent, no chances were taken. In December Chit Hlaing himself, three newspaper editors and a number of others were arrested in advance: 'intimidators' were 'suitably dealt with', in the words of Craddock.[26] It was the tycoon's only experience of prison. The boycott was notably effective at Mandalay (but, under the provisions of the same Act, newspapers were not allowed to report it); elsewhere there were few demonstrations, and cheering crowds were collected to line the railway track.

The National College and a similar establishment at Pakokku had further increased political awareness among monks. For religious reasons they had participated only as observers in GCBA activities. It is alleged that during Chit Hlaing's detention Ba Pe, who remained free, succeeded in persuading the Council to exclude monks entirely, a move that would have slowed the radical trend. When Whyte reported, in June 1922, Chit Hlaing was once more in the chair as the GCBA heard Ba Pe's committee recommend participation in the first real Legislative Council elections. What would have happened cannot be known: after one day the local Commissioner and police chief shut the meeting down. There were more meetings, ever noisier. Chit Hlaing, finding his authority under threat, reversed the decision to exclude the monks, and in fact they were soon to participate as full members. Ba Pe, sensing a whispering campaign against him, broke away, with a group of twenty-one like-minded council members. At the end of the summer there were two rival All Burma conferences. The one organised by the breakaway group became the founding congress of the cleverly-named Twenty-One Party. Naturally it agreed to field candidates for the Legislative Council elections, the issue that Ba Pe's committee had fruitlessly studied. But the rival conference of the GCBA was far better attended. It was addressed for the first time by Ottama, newly freed from gaol; it agreed (in fifteen minutes exactly, said Chit Hlaing triumphantly) to boycott the elections.

When those elections came, in November, Ba Pe's Twenty-One Party fielded candidates and unsurprisingly became the largest party, with 28 of 59 elected seats. The turnout, a bare

7 per cent, shows the sweeping success of the GCBA boycott. At this crucial moment, on 22 December, Craddock's term as Lieutenant-Governor ended. If Simla and London felt that he had failed, this would explain the recall of his predecessor, Harcourt Butler, who served just 12 days before, on 2 January 1923, he was promoted to the rank of Governor. This accorded with Montagu's promise that Burma would become a 'Governor's province' parallel with India.

It was the Governor's prerogative to select his cabinet, and he chose only one councillor from the Twenty-One Party, the rest being loyalists. Interesting, however, in view of Butler's earlier record as an all-out educational imperialist, was the name and portfolio of this one radical. It was Maung Gyi, one of the founders of 1906, henceforth familiarly known as MA Maung Gyi (because he had an MA, and to distinguish him from his loyalist namesake J A Maung Gyi). When the student strike had begun to crumble, towards the end of 1921, the national schools lived on, though almost without resources. It fell to MA Maung Gyi, as Education Minister of the first dyarchy government of Burma, to devise the measure under which some of these independent national schools, an early flowering of Burmese and Buddhist education under British rule, qualified for a share of the budget and a place in the system.

Burmese observers, many of whom regarded Maung Gyi and the whole Twenty-One Party as turncoats, criticised his arrangements as niggardly and restrictive. Craddock, still angry seven years later, dubbed Maung Gyi 'formerly one of the leaders of the boycott' and describes the measure as lacking 'those sound principles which had hitherto always characterised our administration'.[27] In other words, it pleased neither side, like many of the uneasy compromises of Burma's dyarchy. Partial and unsatisfying as they undoubtedly were, these developments of the 1920s and 1930s marked Burma's first steps on the road to independence. Their immediate origins are clear. They lie in the economic upheavals of 1914–18, the concurrent growth of nationalism, and quiet pressure exerted at the right time in the context of the two London delegations of 1919 and 1920. The political atmosphere of 1919 – the talk of 'impartial' resolution of 'all colonial claims' at a Peace Conference at which Burma was not even aware of being represented – may also have had its influence beneath the surface on policy-makers in London and Simla; even, just possibly, in Rangoon.

3

What the Filipinos Ask, 1907–21

In the Philippines, 1907 was a momentous year. The United States had occupied the islands during the Spanish-American War, ending in 1901, and had decided to hold on to them, in spite of unease at the prospect of becoming a colonial power, and in face of determined opposition from the Filipino revolutionaries who fought both Spaniards and Americans for their independence. The governing Philippine Commission, appointed by the United States President and initially led by Governor-General William H Taft, had ruled firmly, without any dangerous challenge, and on the whole benevolently. Among its early legislation, however, was the Sedition Law of November 1901, which, very much as in other colonial administrations, prescribed death or imprisonment for those advocating independence. Although many seemed to accept American rule, the labour men, including the communist leader Crisanto Evangelista and the fiery radical Dominador Gomez, led protests against the government. Born in 1868, Gomez had joined the islands' earliest labour leader, the popular historian Isabelo delos Reyes ('Don Belong'), in founding the Union Obrera Democratica, the 'Workers' Democratic Union' in 1902, soon after the establishment of American civil government. After the first strike, on 2 August of that year, Don Belong went to gaol for sedition and Gomez took on the leadership. After the May Day march in 1903 Gomez himself served a year in prison for sedition.

As in Burma, the Japanese victory against Russia in 1905 reassured those Filipinos who still smarted from their own recent defeat that it was possible, after all, for Asians to win wars. For them, in contrast with the Burmese, a peaceful route towards autonomy had been opened. Almost from the outset, and particularly in the person of Governor-General Taft, American government in the Philippines was notably more enlightened than colonial regimes elsewhere in the region. In 1903, against concerted opposition from American press and business, Taft had made the long-term promise of 'The Philippines for the Filipinos' and his successors began to put it into effect. By 1907 there was discussion in the United States of ultimate independence for the Philippines. Meanwhile the Philippine Organic Act of 1902 laid down that the Commission should eventually become the upper chamber of a legislature whose lower half would be an elected Assembly (whose authority was not extended to non-Christian minority peoples, notably the Muslim 'Moros' of Mindanao and neighbouring smaller islands). This limited form of self-government was to become a reality in 1907.

Campaigning for the first Assembly elections, to be held on 30 July, saw two parties in serious contention, the Nacionalistas and the Progresistas, these being the old Federalistas under a new name. Successive governors had set themselves against early independence and had favoured the Federalistas (whose policy was for the islands to become a state of the United States). The Nacionalistas were an amalgam of earlier small political groups, reconstituted on 12 March 1907 around the policy of 'the immediate independence of the Philippine Islands [as] a free and sovereign nation under a democratic government'.[1]

They were on the way to victory under the efficient leadership of Sergio Osmeña. Just thirty years old, Osmeña was not an unknown quantity; two years earlier, as acting governor of the island province of Cebu, he had organised a welcome for a party of American congressmen led by Taft (who was now United States Secretary of War). It had fallen to Osmeña to present a memorial from the Philippine provinces. 'Designs superior to the will of men have placed the fate of the Filipinos in the hands of the people of the United States. Fortunately the people of the United States have assumed this responsibility,' Osmeña continued carefully, before requesting Congress to 'declare its intention with regard to the future and definite status of the Philippines' and observing that capacity for self-government should be assessed 'from the viewpoint of Philippine interests', not American. That same evening Taft spoke at a banquet, asserting, as he often did, the benefits of progress and the uselessness of political agitation. Philippine leaders, Taft advised, 'should take part in this great work and deal with facts, and not waste their energies and their strength in theories that are impossible'.[2]

The 1907 elections brought sweeping victory in the shape of 59 seats to the Nacionalistas, 16 to their nearest rivals the Progresistas. The turnout was remarkably low, and to at least one observer it appeared that 'most of the Nacionalistas that were elected are more conservative than a number of the Progresista candidates that were defeated'.[3] Osmeña, already well known in the provinces and leader of what was now the majority, was favourite for election as Speaker, leader of the new lower chamber. An old colleague and writer for Osmeña's revolutionary paper *El Nuevo Dia*, Rafael Palma, lobbied hard for him 'among my numerous friends. Most of the delegates were my contemporaries in college, while a few of the younger ones were my students'.[4] Osmeña was challenged for the speakership by the radical Dominador Gomez. The latter, hated by many Americans, was undermined by being forced to submit to re-election following the specious claim that having served in the Spanish army he was a foreign citizen and therefore ineligible for Assembly membership; in this way, Osmeña easily defeated the challenge. He ensured that his friend and future rival, Manuel Quezon, who had given him enthusiastic backing, was elected as majority floor leader, while Palma gained appointment to the upper chamber, the Commission.

These 'new men' of 1907 were little more than schoolboys when Spain began to lose its grip on the Philippines in the mid-1890s. If they served in the revolutionary army, they did so without distinction; after the brief, exciting and difficult independence struggle, each in his own way had found a route forward under American rule. Rafael Palma, a Manila boy born in 1874, studied law at the Dominicans' Universidad de Santo Tomás, the oldest university in Asia, until the war against Spain forced colleges to close. He joined General Antonio Luna's *La Independencia*, and when Luna was assassinated in 1899 Palma himself took over the editorship. The Americans shut the revolutionary paper down in 1900. Palma returned briefly to university to complete his qualification; he met Osmeña there and accepted his invitation to write for the new *El Nuevo Dia* in Cebu.

Sergio Osmeña, four years younger and of Cebuano and Chinese background, an illegitimate child but with wealthy relatives, studied at San Carlos seminary in his native Cebu and then at the Universidad de Santo Tomás; meanwhile, to earn money, he found short-term work in the Spanish administration of Cebu and on local newspapers. In April 1900, now under American rule, he started *El Nuevo Dia*. 'We shall not plant distrust; seeking the national good we shall urge harmony on the two nations,' [5] he wrote in an editorial, but these were censorious days, and the relatively innocuous newspaper was continually being suspended. It failed after a year. Palma went back to Manila to be founding editor of *El Renacimiento*, and Osmeña joined him, but neither was to stay long in journalism. Palma married his proprietor's daughter and took up law again, while Osmeña qualified as a lawyer in 1903, returned to Cebu and began his rapid rise in the provincial administration. By 1906, aged 27, he was provincial governor, one of only five elected in that year who were Nacionalistas.

Manuel Quezon, probably a year older than Osmeña, was also elected in 1905. In ethnic origin he was Spanish and Tagalog (from the majority people of the Manila region). A schoolmaster's son in the remote town of Baler, he walked with his father across the mountains to enrol at San Juan de Letran, where he worked as a teacher's houseboy to pay his fees. He went on to study law at Santo Tomás. He qualified, after the interruption of the war, in 1903; Osmeña was placed second in the bar examination, Quezon fourth, and the bittersweet competition between these two ('little Quezon' always on his mettle, 'frail and slender' Osmeña ever unruffled) would last until the day of Quezon's death 41 years later. He began work in the provincial administration of Tayabas to which his home town belonged. There, just like Osmeña, he rose rapidly, becoming provincial governor in 1906. [6]

The power that Osmeña and the others now gained derived from the silent pact that each had made with the relatively benign American administration. They seemed to accept that independence would come slowly: there is persuasive evidence that Quezon, during the following fifteen years, was keen to hold back the pace of independence.[7] During the first session of the Assembly after the election in 1907, in spite of their election platform, the Nacionalistas never allowed a motion in favour of independence; Quezon, Osmeña's lieutenant, was even ready to assist Commissioner Cameron Forbes with legislation that the administration needed – an arrangement that improved the standing of Forbes (soon to be Governor-General) in the eyes of Secretary of War Taft (soon to be President). Quezon, Forbes reported, was 'without exception the most useful man to the Government ... I do not know what I should have done without him.'[8]

But they had not given up their ultimate aim of independence: 'This ideal has not dimmed, not even at the moment of taking the oath of allegiance,' said Osmeña in winding up the Assembly's first session.[9] The second election in 1909 brought an even more crushing Nacionalista victory: they won 62 seats to the Progresistas' 17. Ten days later a new Governor-General took office, the last in a series of Republicans. In his approach to his task Cameron Forbes (see sidebar, p 58) 'concentrated on economic advancement ... and left the islands with a splendid system of highways,' an American observer wrote drily,[10] pointedly omitting any praise of Forbes's political actions. A Filipino author puts the matter more bluntly: Forbes 'had no sympathy with the ideal of independence and frankly announced that his policy was that of economic development. He was even willing to curtail the appropriations for schools so that he could carry on his policy.'[11]

Forbes's policy was heartily approved by American businessmen, but it outraged the Nacionalistas. Rapidly exhausting the goodwill of the Assembly, he was soon unable to get his legislation passed except when Osmeña agreed to help; thus, ironically, Osmeña and the Nacionalistas gained from Forbes's intransigence. In a curious sense Osmeña became Forbes's patron. A contemporary commentator makes the position clear. 'The Filipinos regarded [Osmeña] as the real head of the government … the Governor-General can not properly be criticized for showing undue deference to the speaker and his party: it was necessary in order to secure legislation which was required to carry out [his] policy.' [12]

Commission and Assembly, upper and lower house, each elected a resident commissioner to represent the Philippines in the American House of Representatives. In 1909 the Commission elected Manuel Quezon. Washington was not new to him (he had visited both Russia and the United States on a fact-finding tour in 1908); he settled in and got down to work, but his maiden speech in the House came only on 14 May 1910. It was a measured survey – a surprise to those who expected passion from Washington's first Filipino nationalist – balancing the American administration's achievements against its growing unpopularity. It filled in what the administration's publicity left unsaid, and prepared the new Secretary of War, Jacob N Dickinson, for what would face him in September on the almost-obligatory visit to the Philippines, the United States' most extensive overseas possession. Osmeña, still Speaker, had ready for him a 'Political Memorial on Immediate Independence'; more significant, Forbes's manoeuvres had driven the Nacionalistas into agreement with the opposition on the issue of a constitution. 'Whatever may be the ultimate and definite political status of the country and whether we secure independence immediately or some time later, it is evident the the Filipino people need at this very moment a constitution.' [13]

This petition was presented to the Secretary of War together by Osmeña and the rival Progresista leader, Vicente Singson Encarnacion.

There was a long and dangerous stand-off. By 1912 Forbes was suffering from 'breakdown due to overwork in the islands'.[14] The stalemate was ended in Washington by the election first of a Democratic majority in the House, and shortly afterwards of a Democratic President, Woodrow Wilson. Democrats in general (and Wilson in particular) were unhappy with the notion of the United States as a colonial power. Wilson was prepared to act in accord with this conviction; he listened to Quezon on the choice of a new Governor-General, and it was as a result of Quezon's objections to a different candidate that the liberal Congressman Francis Burton Harrison had a meeting with Quezon on 18 August 1913 and was faced with the question, 'Why shouldn't *you* be Governor-General yourself?'[15] An objection to Harrison, raised by former Governor Taft, was his exciting private life (his current wife had divorced her previous husband a few hours before their marriage).[16] Wilson stood out for Quezon's choice, which other advisers supported. Harrison was appointed, and, as with Forbes, it may be said that Quezon in this way became Harrison's patron. One observer even found it necessary to contradict 'the popular belief that [Harrison] was but a pliable tool in Filipino hands'.[17]

Harrison's speech on arrival at Manila on 6 October 1913 signalled rapid change: 'People of the Philippine Islands! A new era is dawning! We place within your reach the instruments of your redemption … Under Divine Providence the event is in your hands.'[18] Whether Harrison knew that he was echoing the words of the Hongkong Junta fifteen years earlier, he does not say. There was an immediate change in substance: he announced that the appointed upper house, the Commission, would henceforth have a Filipino majority. The selection of commissioners was agreed with Osmeña.

It finally included Rafael Palma, reappointed alongside Jaime de Veyra and the Progresista leader Vicente Singson Encarnacion. Harrison also pressed swiftly ahead with the policy (suspended under Forbes) of increasing the proportion of Filipinos in government service. He became, and remained, deeply unpopular with Americans in the islands, mostly businesspeople and government employees. The livelihood of these latter was directly threatened by Harrison's policy. By the same token, his popularity among Filipinos was high, though opposition parties could be heard to complain that it was the Nacionalistas that he always consulted.

In spite of these rapid changes, the unrepentant revolutionary Artemio Ricarte y Garcia chose Christmas 1914 as the moment to stir up an anti-American rebellion. Alone among those captured in 1900, he continued to refuse the oath of allegiance to the US. Thus on release from Bilibid goal in 1910 he had been exiled to Hong Kong. He now secretly returned to the Philippines. American newspapers, generally unfavourable to Harrison's administration, carried stories of widespread disturbances for

Jaime C de Veyra (1873–1963), was born in Leyte island, and attended the Dominican college of San Juan de Letran and Universidad de Santo Tomás in Manila. A civil servant under the last Spanish governor of Leyte, he joined Osmeña on *El Nuevo Dia* and afterwards on Cebu municipal council. He was elected governor of Leyte in 1906; Member of the Assembly in 1907; commissioner 1913–16; resident commissioner in Washington 1917–23, and afterwards he became a Philippine historian.

Artemio Ricarte y Garcia (1866–1945) fought for Philippine independence; captured by Americans in 1900, he refused to take an oath of allegiance to the US. He was imprisoned until 1910, then exiled to Hong Kong. He later lived in Japan and he flew to the Philippines under Japanese occupation to organise resistance against the returning Americans. He died of dysentery the year the Second World War ended.

several days around Christmas; this was an exaggeration.[19] The actual uprising on the morning of 25 December was a fiasco, resulting in twenty arrests. Ricarte was deported to Shanghai.

In the meantime, although things were moving in the Philippines, there was increasing demand for legislation – to render eventual Philippine independence certain and, some would add, to bring it closer. This US legislation took a tortuous path. Representative William A Jones, Democrat chairman of the House Committee on Insular Affairs, put a bill forward in March 1912 that proposed independence in 1921. It stalled, but Quezon continued to lobby for it assiduously in personal contacts and in the monthly magazine *The Filipino People* that he published from the resident commissioner's office. Wilson having now taken office as President, the Jones Bill reappeared in revised form in 1914, this time without an independence deadline. 'It is, as it has always been, the purpose of the people of the United States [so the preamble asserted] to withdraw their sovereignty over the Philippine Islands and to recognize their independence as soon as a stable government can be established therein'; the bill set up means to the end of 'stable government' by revising the *de facto* constitution of the Philippines, and notably by replacing the appointed Commission with an almost wholly elected upper house, a Senate. On the issue of independence, however, Republicans were cold and even Democrats found it difficult to agree, as shown by the failure of the provocative Clarke Amendment which would have restored the fixed independence timetable that had been omitted from the revised Jones Bill.[20] In early 1915 President Wilson apologised to Harrison and Quezon for the delay to the Jones Bill caused by Republicans 'who would yield only if we withdrew the assurance of ultimate independence contained in the preamble. That we would not do. The bill will have my support until it passes',[21] he promised. Only on 29 August 1916 did it finally pass.

Jones himself, in debate in the House, claimed that his bill 'virtually places it in the power of the Philippine people to say when they shall receive … independence'.[22] Jones exaggerated, and the bill was not enough to meet the stated aim of the Nacionalista party, which continued to be formulated as immediate independence. Quezon wrote: 'We accept the Jones Bill, but we hold fast to our program – unalterable, unassailable, and permanent as it is.'[23] While asserting, dubiously, that independence had always been America's purpose, the Law posed a new question. If, before independence was recognised, a 'stable government' must have been established, how would this be shown?

> 'It is, as it has always been, the purpose of the people of the United States to withdraw their sovereignty over the Philippine Islands and to recognize their independence as soon as a stable government can be established therein.'
>
> PHILIPPINE AUTONOMY ACT (JONES LAW), 1916

In October 1916 the Nacionalistas did even better than before in the Philippine elections, winning 22 of 24 Senate seats and 75 of 90 seats in the lower house (henceforth the House of Representatives). The Governor being now so favourable to the Nacionalistas, there was in fact no political room for the traditionally pro-American Progresistas, and the two were soon to merge. Quezon, having reliquished his position in Washington, was now elected to the Senate (and became its president) while Osmena remained speaker of the House. The following January a cabinet was formed, almost wholly of elected representatives. It included Rafael Palma as Secretary of the Interior, Dionisio Jakosalem (who had been Osmeña's successor as governor of Cebu) in charge of commerce and

PRESIDENT WILSON'S FOURTEEN POINTS, 8 JANUARY 1918

The program of the world's peace, therefore, is our program; and that program, the only possible program, as we see it, is this:

I. Open covenants of peace, openly arrived at, after which there shall be no private international understandings of any kind but diplomacy shall proceed always frankly and in the public view.

II. Absolute freedom of navigation upon the seas, outside territorial waters, alike in peace and in war, except as the seas may be closed in whole or in part by international action for the enforcement of international covenants.

III. The removal, so far as possible, of all economic barriers and the establishment of an equality of trade conditions among all the nations consenting to the peace and associating themselves for its maintenance.

IV. Adequate guarantees given and taken that national armaments will be reduced to the lowest point consistent with domestic safety.

V. A free, open-minded, and absolutely impartial adjustment of all colonial claims, based upon a strict observance of the principle that in determining all such questions of sovereignty the interests of the populations concerned must have equal weight with the equitable claims of the government whose title is to be determined.

VI. The evacuation of all Russian territory and such a settlement of all questions affecting Russia as will secure the best and freest cooperation of the other nations of the world in obtaining for her an unhampered and unembarrassed opportunity for the independent determination of her own political development and national policy and assure her of a sincere welcome into the society of free nations under institutions of her own choosing; and, more than a welcome, assistance also of every kind that she may need and may herself desire. The treatment accorded Russia by her sister nations in the months to come will be the acid test of their good will, of their comprehension of her needs as distinguished from their own interests, and of their intelligent and unselfish sympathy.

VII. Belgium, the whole world will agree, must be evacuated and restored, without any attempt to limit the sovereignty which she enjoys in common with all other free nations. No other single act will serve as this will serve to restore confidence among the nations in the laws which they have themselves set and determined for the government of their relations with one another. Without this healing act the whole structure and validity of international law is forever impaired.

VIII. All French territory should be freed and the invaded portions restored, and the wrong done to France by Prussia in 1871 in the matter of Alsace-Lorraine, which has unsettled the peace of the world for nearly fifty years, should be righted, in order that peace may once more be made secure in the interest of all.

IX. A readjustment of the frontiers of Italy should be effected along clearly recognizable lines of nationality.

X. The peoples of Austria-Hungary, whose place among the nations we wish to see safeguarded and assured, should be accorded the freest opportunity to autonomous development.

XI. Rumania, Serbia, and Montenegro should be evacuated; occupied territories restored; Serbia accorded free and secure access to the sea; and the relations of the several Balkan states to one another determined by friendly counsel along historically established lines of allegiance and nationality; and international guarantees of the political and economic independence and territorial integrity of the several Balkan states should be entered into.

XII. The Turkish portion of the present Ottoman Empire should be assured a secure sovereignty, but the other nationalities which are now under Turkish rule should be assured an undoubted security of life and an absolutely unmolested opportunity of autonomous development, and the Dardanelles should be permanently opened as a free passage to the ships and commerce of all nations under international guarantees.

XIII. An independent Polish state should be erected which should include the territories inhabited by indisputably Polish populations, which should be assured a free and secure access to the sea, and whose political and economic independence and territorial integrity should be guaranteed by international covenant.

XIV. A general association of nations must be formed under specific covenants for the purpose of affording mutual guarantees of political independence and territorial integrity to great and small states alike.

communication, and just one American, Charles Yeater, as Secretary of Information.

The first steps in demonstrating readiness for independence, as prompted by the Jones Law, were taken only in 1919. The delay occurred because the United States had joined the European war in April 1917. The Philippines were so far distant from the war zone that the islands were scarcely involved in any direct way, but Philippine politicians did not wish to be, or to be seen as, an unwanted distraction in wartime. They held back, therefore; but close attention was paid in the Philippines when in January 1918 President Wilson outlined America's aims, with a view to the eventual peace terms, in his Fourteen Points. The fifth of these called for 'a free, open-minded, and absolutely impartial adjustment of all colonial claims' with reference to 'the interests of the populations concerned'. This appeared to chime extremely well with the wishes of Filipinos as represented by the Nacionalista party.

No sooner had the war ended on 11 November 1918 than the upper and lower house agreed that an Independence Mission should go to Washington to put their case. The leader was Quezon; along with Governor Harrison he was in New York at the time, but this did not prevent his selecting his colleagues by a series of telegrams to Manila. The mission eventually included two members of the cabinet, Rafael Palma (who was entrusted with leading the team till Quezon rejoined it) and Dionisio Jakosalem; and another senator, the former Progresista leader Vicente Singson Encarnacion. Maximo Kalaw, writer on Philippine politics and until recently Quezon's private secretary, was appointed secretary to the Mission. In Manila, in advance of departure, no publicity at all was allowed: the names of the team were made public only three days before sailing, and they were told to refuse all invitations by politicians and journalists.

Charles Yeater, acting Governor-General, acknowledged that they showed 'exceptional discretion'.[24]

By a succession of telegrams Wilson delayed the first mission's departure from Manila until 14 February 1919. At the end of 1918 he was too busy with preparations for the Paris Peace Conference, which was to begin in January and at which, thanks to his Fourteen Points, the issues of self-determination and of colonial claims were to be on the agenda.

Wilson intended, no doubt, to be back in Washington, his business in Paris completed, in the late spring. Realising eventually that the Conference would drag on, he decided that he had to return to Washington – to adjourn Congress and deal with urgent business – before a second session in Paris. It was by then too late, and in any case politically impossible, to delay the Philippine mission any further; thus, leaving the Conference on 15 February almost at the same moment that the mission left Manila, Wilson did what he had to do in the United States and set out in haste for Paris again (arriving there on 13 March) before Quezon and his colleagues reached Washington. They never met Wilson at all.

They were overtaken on their journey to Washington by two long telegrams. The first, containing a Declaration of Purposes, had been agreed by upper and lower houses on 8 March; it set out the case for independence. The second, a postscript dated 17 March, was evidently a response to news of the Peace Conference discussions concerning the projected League of Nations. It suggested how the Philippines, when independent, might play its part in international guarantees of the independence of weak nations within the new world order that President Wilson and his allies were establishing in Paris.

Quezon met his colleagues when they disembarked in San Francisco. He now took charge of the mission, whose publicity continued to be very carefully managed. Kalaw compiled a forty-page *Guide Book on the Philippine Question* for publication in Washington and circulated it to the press and politicians. In Wilson's absence the initial statement of the Philippines case was made to James Baker, Secretary of War, on 4 April; Harrison was present, as was Jaime de Veyra, one of the two resident commissioners in Washington. Baker spoke briefly in response and handed over a letter from the President. 'The Filipino people shall not be absent from my thoughts,' Wilson wrote. 'Not the least important labor of the conference which now requires my attendance is that of making the pathway of the weaker people of the world less perilous – a labor which should be, and doubtless is, of deep and abiding interest to the Filipino people.' This happened to match almost perfectly the mission's own instructions (if one discounted the implication that the Filipinos were among the weaker people of the world) and it was accompanied by warm wishes for their success. The end of their labours, Wilson wrote vaguely, was 'almost in sight'.[25]

This meeting was followed by a busy programme of social events (during which Kalaw's article 'What the Filipinos Ask' appeared in the *New York Times* on 18 May). Governor Harrison's mother, the novelist Constance Cary, welcomed the mission at a reception in Washington. Meanwhile, Harrison's personal life distracted attention. At noon on 15 May, in San Diego, his wife divorced him; at 5.30 p.m. on the same day, in Chicago, he married again. Beth Wrentmore, his third wife, was an eighteen-year-old University of California student, and the marriage was said 'in the public press' to have taken place against her parents' wishes: Baker, reporting this confidentially to Wilson, asked whether Harrison should be prevented from returning to the strongly Catholic Philippines, where, he supposed, the divorce would be frowned on. President Wilson, preoccupied by the Greek invasion of Smyrna which happened on the same day and for which he bore heavy responsibility, took the news more calmly.

The really serious item on the mission's timetable was a joint hearing on 2 June before the House and Senate Committees on Insular Affairs. The international context was well stated by the Republican (but progressive) Representative John I Nolan, whose words are good evidence that in 1919 the talk of freedom for former Turkish, Austrian and German territories was seen as having implications for others too. 'Your idea is that if we try to apply the principle of self-determination ... to all the rest of the world, we ought to be in a position now to apply it to our own territory.' 'Exactly,' said Quezon. Beyond generalities, however, some awkward questions faced Quezon and his colleagues. The Philippines had no army: did they want to be 'wholly severed from' the United States, asked Senator Warren Harding, or would they expect American protection even when nominally independent? After some inconclusive fencing on this point, Quezon finally offered an answer in three steps: 'I think that the independence of the Philippines under the League [of Nations] is what ... appeals to everybody ... but if there be no League the Filipinos would like to see independence ... guaranteed by international agreement ... but if that should not be possible, they want independence anyway.'[26] The difficulty was that the League, Wilson's favourite child, was becoming daily

REPRESENTATIVE JOHN I NOLAN: 'Your idea is that if we try to apply the principle of self-determination ... to all the rest of the world, we ought to be in a position now to apply it to our own territory.'

MANUEL L QUEZON: 'Exactly.'

JOINT HEARING BEFORE THE HOUSE AND SENATE COMMITTEES ON INSULAR AFFAIRS, 2 JUNE, 1919 less popular in Washington. Quezon was clearly well aware of the problem, but, as an outsider, he could hardly speak openly about it.

Uncertainty on this issue suggested a supplementary question: how would the Philippines defend themselves if threatened by an Asian power, for example Japan? A Democrat, Senator James Phelan, led Quezon into the admission that Japanese immigration, a growing problem unlikely to be solved by Philippine independence, could lead to economic and even political domination.

After the meeting, at which Harrison was said to have made a 'wonderful impression', Quezon rewarded the governor by writing personally to Wilson to recommend that Harrison retain the governorship. There was no scandal beyond what the press had created, he said; even that was now forgotten.[28]

Policy-makers in Washington, though conscious of the difficult issues before them, regarded them as solvable; what they needed was a lead from Wilson. Baker wrote on 8 June to the leading Democrat Finis J Garrett: 'Off hand, I should say that the thing to do would be to fix a definite date in the future at which independence should be declared, and if I were writing the resolution

THE LEAGUE OF NATIONS
The League of Nations had its origins in thinking during the war about the future shape of international relations, not least in President Woodrow Wilson's Fourteen Points of 8 January 1918, which called, *inter alia*, for a 'general association of nations'. The Covenant of the League of Nations was adopted at the Paris Peace Conference, and the League came into existence on 10 January 1920, with its headquarters at Geneva. Its effectiveness was undermined from the start when on 19 November 1919, the American Senate refused to ratify the Peace Treaty, and the United States did not join. The League was responsible for the Mandates system for the former German and Ottoman territories, and hence for Britain's Mandate for Palestine. When the United Nations Organization was founded in 1945, it became redundant and formally went out of existence the following year.[27]

at this minute I would say ... 1925, and the people of the Philippine Islands ... in the meantime should ... select a popular constitutional convention and adopt a constitution (it may be, however, that the President has an entirely different idea on this subject as the result of his conferences abroad), and I would suggest that you and I take the matter up with him on his return, which cannot in any case be long delayed.'[29] So it stood when the members of the mission left Washington. Wilson was still in Paris, impatient to be gone.

He left on the evening of 28 June, the very day on which he, his allies and his defeated enemy had signed the Treaty of Versailles. Back at home he threw himself into political campaigning and the defence of the League of Nations, with no time to spare for the Philippines. On 25 September, while campaigning in Colorado, he suffered a devastating stroke from which he never fully recovered. The projected discussion with Baker and Garrett was never held.

Members of the Independence Mission returned to Manila during July and August; Quezon, who travelled on the ss *Empress of Russia*, was already home by 2 July. Although there had been pointed questioning by members of the Committees on Insular Affairs, overall they were well satisfied. They had failed to meet Wilson, and Wilson's words on the issue of Philippine independence had been notably vague (whether by accident or design) but that hardly mattered since Secretary of War Baker had been businesslike and favourable in his approach both to the general issue and to the question of timing. It seemed clear that he spoke for the President.

Legislation on the Philippine issue was put forward in Congress in late 1919 and 1920 but made no progress. Wilson, indeed, in his farewell message, assured Congress that the Philippines 'have succeeded in maintaining a stable government

William Cameron Forbes (1870–1959). Philippines commissioner from 1904, Governor-General 1909–13; promoted economic development against political change. Joint author of Forbes-Wood report, 1921; US ambassador to Japan, 1930–32. He wrote *The Philippine Islands* (1945).

Francis Burton Harrison (1873–1957) was born in New York City. An aristocratic and wealthy Democrat politician, he was Governor-General of Philippines 1913–21. He favoured rapid reform, writing *The Corner-Stone of Philippine Independence* (1922). After 1935 he served as adviser to Manuel Quezon and subsequent Philippine leaders. He died in New Jersey and was buried in Manila.

Charles Yeater (1861–1943) was born in Missouri. He spoke in 1889 on 'The Influence of the West on Nationalism'. Secretary of Information and deputy Governor-General of the Philippines under Harrison, he became acting Governor-General in 1921.

Leonard Wood (1860–1927) was born in New Hampshire. A career soldier, he fought in Cuba and (fiercely) in the Philippines. He became governor of Moro province 1903; Chief of Staff 1910; candidate for Republican presidential nomination 1920; joint author of Forbes-Wood report 1921; and Governor-General from 1921 until his death in 1927.

since the last action of Congress in their behalf … I respectfully recommend that [we] keep our promise to the people of these islands by granting them the independence which they honorably covet.'[30] But (as everyone knew by this time) Wilson was to be succeeded as President on 4 March 1921 by his bitter political opponent, the Republican Senator Harding, the same Harding who had demanded to know whether the Philippine mission aimed at 'complete severance' from the United States and whose firm view was that it would be contrary to American interests to encourage any such thing.

One day after Harding's inauguration Francis Harrison was replaced as Governor-General of the Philippines (his temporary successor was his deputy, Charles Yeater). Harding lost no time in sending out a Philippine mission of his own, a team of two who were to make a fresh judgment on the independence question. The choice of these advisers left little doubt as to the decision they were expected to reach. They were former governor Cameron Forbes, noted during his term of office for having stalled and even reversed the progress towards Philippine autonomy; and a fine old soldier, Leonard Wood, admired in the United States, but infamous in the Philippines for his ruthlessness twenty years earlier during the Spanish-American War. The Forbes-Wood report advised that recent liberalism had been economically damaging and that the time was not ripe for independence (adding insult to injury, the public funding of missions to Washington was now ruled illegal). His task completed, Wood himself was now nominated by Harding as Governor-General. Harrison, with his young wife and their new-born child, left the Philippines at once, living for the next fifteen years in Scotland and Morocco and withdrawing totally from politics. He never said why. Relevant, surely, were sustained and vitriolic attacks on him in the US and the English-language Philippine press, sniping over his private life, criticism in the Forbes-Wood report and an already-breaking scandal of confusion, incompetence and fraud at the Philippines National Bank.

In early 1919, when Wilson as US President and Harrison as Governor-General had been equally insistent on rapid progress to independence for the Philippines, it could not reasonably have been predicted that the Independence Mission would fail so comprehensively. The scene was set for a more-or-less annual series of eleven further missions to the United States between 1922 and 1933, financed by voluntary contributions from Filipinos; and for twenty-two more years of rivalry between Sergio Osmeña and Manuel Quezon, both of them determined to lead the Philippines to freedom.

4

National and Colonial Questions: Indonesia, 1908–27

In January 1918 President Wilson had called for 'impartial adjustment of all colonial claims' and for attention to 'the interests of the populations concerned'. The expectation that these words aroused, among peoples far distant from the war zone of the First World War and never ruled by the defeated powers, were real, and they were not to be resolved by the Paris Peace Conference. While it pursued its course, in March 1919 Lenin was able to announce at the founding congress of the Communist International: 'We have here quite a number of representatives of the revolutionary movement in the colonial and backward countries … The important thing is that a beginning has been made … We see taking place a union between revolutionary proletarians of the capitalist, advanced countries, and the … oppressed masses of colonial, Eastern countries.'[1]

Hồ Chí Minh moved on, in two years, from the expectations embodied in his 1919 Paris *Revendications*; in 1921 he began his ultimately successful tussles in Moscow to get Comintern backing for resistance in Vietnam. To those pressing for freedom for the Dutch Indies, Paris never seemed relevant; the Netherlands, a neutral state in the First World War now providing sanctuary to the defeated Kaiser Wilhelm II, was not even present at the Conference. It can be no surprise that Henk Sneevliet, founder of the *Indische Sociaal-Democratische Vereniging (*Indies Social-Democratic Association), and his ally Semaun, who in 1921 would become chairman of *Perserikatan Kommunist di Hindia (the* Indies Communist Association), looked to Moscow, and not to Paris, in their struggle against colonial rule.

By the beginning of the 20th century the Indies – the islands of modern Indonesia – were firmly under Netherlands control. Local wars and insurrections were practically at an end; Aceh, in northern Sumatra, was the last to fall, and by about 1904 even it had been forced into submission. It was to 1908 that Semaun, in an historical survey of the origins of communism in his native Indonesia delivered to the First Congress of the Workers of the East in 1922, dated the real beginnings of the new independence movement in the Dutch Indies. The conditions for discontent, he explained, had been created by burgeoning capitalist investment; then Japan's victory in 1905 gave 'new strength to the ambitions of the native upper classes, among which they crystallized into a nationalist mood'.[2] Although a communist speaking to communists, Semaun was being objective: 1908 saw the foundation by students in Batavia (Jakarta) of the first identifiably nationalist group, *Budi Utomo (*High Endeavour), a non-communist Islamic educational and self-improvement group. Budi Utomo spread rapidly across Java but remained almost apolitical, confining itself to submitting petitions when administrative regulations were in opposition to religious rule or custom. In the same year the *Indische Vereeniging (*Indies Society) was founded by Indonesian students in the Netherlands; it, too, was to have its influence in later years.

The next milestone year was 1912, which saw the foundation of two political organisations. The *Indische Partij* (Indies Party), was open to Indonesians but really aimed to represent the interests of Eurasians, those of mixed Dutch-Indonesian descent, against newly-arrived European migrant workers: 'the Indies for those who make their home there' was its keynote.[3] It was radical, indeed sympathetic to Marxism, and was suppressed just a year later by the colonial administration, whose Governor-General at the time was the conservative AWF Idenburg. The founders of the Indische Partij were exiled. This measure, which excluded them from the Indies while allowing them to live freely in the Netherlands (or elsewhere), was to become typical of the Dutch Indies administration; it led to a rapid turnover of nationalist party leaders. In its founders' absence, the Indische Partij regrouped as *Insulinde*, continued to speak for Eurasians and made no move to broaden its appeal.

The other new organisation of 1912 was *Sarekat Islam*, the Muslim Society, a political grouping aimed specifically at Muslim native Indonesians. In attempting to emasculate Sarekat Islam, which potentially had a far more widespread constituency than the Indische Partij, Idenburg chose a different method: local groups were permitted to form but a national association was at first forbidden. Youngest of the early leaders was Tjokroaminoto, scion of a noble Javanese family, who worked in a sugar factory near Surabaya and was recruited to join the nascent organisation in late 1911. He was well placed to become chairman, aged thirty-three, when a *Centraal Sarekat Islam* was eventually permitted in 1915; he was at the fore at the first national congress in Bandung in 1916, and led Sarekat Islam and its successor parties until his early death in 1934. A special quality of his, rare in the region in the early 1900s, was the refusal of colonial deference, the conviction that Indonesians were the equal of Europeans.[4] He never spoke for violent resistance, however. Sarekat Islam, in his words, aimed to 'build nationalism, recover the human rights that God granted'; yet he insisted that 'Islamic *shari'a* tells us to obey the order of the Dutch government'.[5]

It was the addition to this nascent nationalism of an active trade union movement that would begin to provoke real change. This development largely coincided with the arrival of Henk Sneevliet in the Dutch Indies from the Netherlands. A former railwayman and union activist bearing bruises from the internecine disputes of Dutch socialists and workers, Sneevliet – who was to be Semaun's mentor – is described by a friend as 'a typical Dutchman ... well-nourished with plenty of milk products and a pink and white face, round like the full moon'.[6] Sneevliet, then aged thirty, needed to make a fresh start in the Indies, and took the capitalist shilling as secretary to the Semarang Trade Federation. Yet within a year he had added to his interests the editorship of *Orgaan*, the newspaper of the rail workers' union based at Semarang. He renamed it *De Volharding* ('Persistence'), and his egalitarian influence was crucial in turning the originally Eurasian union into something unique in the Indies – a union that crossed racial lines, was increasingly steered by its Indonesian majority (to the point where Europeans and Eurasians began to leave it) and persuaded its employer to take the rare step of offering equal pay for equal work. Semaun, aged fifteen, had joined the union's Surabaya branch in 1914. He found a full-time post at union headquarters and started the paper's Malay edition *Si Tetap* ('Mr Persistent'), neatly adapting the title of the Dutch edition. At almost the same moment he was elected secretary of the Semarang Sarekat Islam.

DUTCH INDIES COMMUNIST LEADERS

Henk Sneevliet (pseudonym Maring) (1883–1942) was a communist trade union activist in the Netherlands and Dutch Indies, whence he was expelled in 1918. Prominent at the Second Comintern Congress in 1920, he worked in China 1921–3, then returned to the Netherlands. He resisted the German occupation, but was captured and executed at Amersfoort in 1942.

Semaun or Semaoen (c. 1898–1971) was a union activist and journalist. Joint founder and chairman of the Indonesian Communist Party (PKI) 1920, he attended the First Congress of the Workers of the East in 1922. Expelled from the Dutch Indies in 1923, he attended the Fifth Comintern Congress in 1924. He returned to Indonesia in 1956.

Dolf Baars (known as Asser Baars) (1892–1944) taught engineering and was a communist journalist and editor of *Het Vrije Woord*. Joint founder of PKI, he was expelled from the Dutch Indies in 1921. He worked in Russia as an engineer until 1927, then returned to the Netherlands, turning against Communism. Under the German occupation, he was deported to Auschwitz and died there in 1944.

Darsono (Raden Darsono Notosudirdjo) (1893–1976) was a teacher and journalist. Joint founder of PKI, he attended the Third Comintern Congress in 1921. He was arrested in 1925, and expelled from the Dutch Indies in 1926. Adviser to the Indonesian Foreign Ministry from 1950, he died in 1976.

Sneevliet's political activity ranged beyond the union. In May 1914 he called a meeting at Surabaya of socialist sympathisers, nearly all of them Dutch or Eurasian, at which it was agreed to found the *Indische Sociaal-Democratische Vereniging,* the Indies Social-Democratic Association (ISDV). Although not assertively Marxist at this point, the ISDV had a Marxist core. It began a newspaper, *Het Vrije Woord* ('The Free Word'); Asser Baars, a Marxist engineering teacher recently arrived from the Netherlands, was a leading writer for this paper and eventually its editor. As the association's guiding light, Sneevliet urged the need to form alliances with other anti-capitalist groups (or, using a later term, to infiltrate them). Insulinde was the first and easiest target, but as a Eurasian interest group Insulinde could never be a real mass movement. By 1916, therefore, Sneevliet was pressing for close involvement with Sarekat Islam, now a sprawling, decentralised organisation of over 300,000 members. In so doing he relied on Semaun, who was popular in Sarekat Islam, and as a Javanese of Islamic background was just the man to persuade his contemporaries to join the ISDV while remaining in Sarekat Islam. Thus, by way of its Semarang branch and of increasing shared membership with the originally tiny ISDV, the whole Sarekat Islam found itself swaying towards a radical and Marxist viewpoint.

A wave of strikes in 1917 and 1918 was sparked by rapidly-increasing poverty and insecurity, both rural and urban, and especially among factory workers. The Dutch Indies was suffering, albeit indirectly, the effects of the First World War; official neutrality was no protection, for the Netherlands themselves or their colonial territories, against economic disruption. In this unsettled atmosphere, news of revolution in Russia led Henk Sneevliet to speak out more boldly than before on the need for revolution in the Dutch Indies. He was briefly arrested. He had in any case gone too far for the moderates in the ISDV; their resignations left the organisation more radical than ever.

It fell to Idenburg's successor as Governor-General, JP van Limburg Stirum, to preside over a novel experiment for the Dutch Indies, the Volksraad. This was superficially not unlike an elected legislature, but half its members were appointed by the Governor and it lacked the right to legislate. Sarekat Islam, being by far the largest political grouping in the Indies and sympathetic to the majority population group, was bound to be well represented in the 1918 elections to the first Volksraad. The ISDV, by contrast, stood aloof; now unanimously Marxist and intent on revolution, it put no candidates forward for election and it talked of disrupting the Volksraad's activities if any of its representatives were appointed. These proved to be tactical errors. Tjokroaminoto, leader of Sarekat Islam, had been finding it hard to keep his organisation together in face of agitation from extremist members to support the strikes in 1917 and 1918. It was all too obvious that Sneevliet and Baars were at the root of the trouble; some even suspected that they were colonialist plants, intended from the first to weaken Sarekat Islam.[7] Perhaps it was to test this theory that Sarekat Islam – well-behaved and constructive participant in the Volksraad – now put pressure on the Governor-General to do something about Sneevliet.

At this moment, in November 1918, came news from the Netherlands that the activist Pieter Jelles Troelstra had proclaimed a socialist revolution. Again Sneevliet and the ISDV responded at once, but the uprisings they attempted in the army came to nothing; and it was soon known that the Netherlands revolution had not happened after all. Van Limburg Stirum now had every excuse to do what Sarekat Islam had suggested: Sneevliet was arrested, tried on a charge of sedition, and exiled in December 1918. He retreated to the Netherlands, where, finding the Communist Party unwelcoming, he set to work in the trade union movement there, though he also retained his association with the ISDV.

Baars and Semaun, who retained his popularity within Sarekat Islam despite the long-running disputes, remained and soon dominated the ISDV. They were now joined by another fiery journalist, Darsono, who had come to prominence during the strikes. A police chief's son who began his career as a teacher of agriculture, he had heard Sneevliet speak in his own defence during his trial in Semarang, and was converted to communism. In his paper *Sinar Hindia*, Darsono now tapped the hidden vein of ethnic nationalism by attacking Chinese workers: 'behaving like cowards', he said, they had caused the strike to fail.[8]

Meanwhile in Paris the Peace Conference opened in January 1919; and in March the Third International (or Communist International, or Comintern) was founded in Moscow. It aimed to replace the Second or Socialist International, the earlier grouping of socialist and labour parties, with a much tighter and more single-minded union of communist parties. With Lenin's *Imperializm, kak noveyshy etap kapitalizma* ('Imperialism as the newest stage of capitalism') (1917) as one of its textbooks, the Comintern had the theoretical underpinning for an interest in revolution in the colonies, anathema to several participants at the Paris Peace Conference and a notable blind spot for members of the Second International.

> 'Java is the land of our forefathers. We are the householders, but we are pushed aside by the guests.'
>
> DARSONO QUOTED IN SINAR HINDIA (31 OCTOBER 1918)[9]

The Comintern set up a West European Bureau which in early 1920 held a conference in Amsterdam. Sneevliet attended it as representative of the ISDV and, so he asserted, of Sarekat Islam too, reporting on the advance of trade unionism and communism in the Indies as well as he could without up-to-date news. News of these events spread widely. In the Dutch Indies, at a May 1920 congress under the management of Asser Baars, the ISDV determined to reform itself as *Perserikatan Kommunist di Hindia* (PKI), Indies Communist Association, with Semaun as chairman, and to join the Comintern. As we have seen, at its congress at Tours at the end of the year the French socialist party, in the presence of Hô Chí Minh, would take the same step. Hence at the second Comintern congress, in

July 1920, there were to be a few representatives of communist parties from colonial territories.

Hô had been variously introduced during his time in France: 'secretary of the Vietnamese Socialist Party' at a rally in Paris; 'the Indochina delegate' at Tours. In Moscow, too, affiliations were not always what they seemed. Manabendra Nath Roy represented India, though since there was as yet no Indian communist party he attended as a delegate of the Mexican Communist Party. Sneevliet (though Dutch by birth and forbidden to return to Indonesia) came to speak for the Indonesian communist movement to which he had devoted so many years of work. This would have meant the new PKI, had he known it existed, but the news of its founding had not yet reached Europe. Since Comintern bureaucracy demanded accreditation, he talked his way in with the papers he still retained from 1919.

There was to be plenary debate on communist tactics in 'colonial and oppressed countries'. In early June, in advance of the congress, Lenin circulated his *Draft Theses on National and Colonial Questions* (the programme that, translated into French, inspired Hô Chí Minh). In the preface to the new French and German editions of his re-titled *Imperializm kak vysšaja stadija kapitalizma* ('Imperialism as the highest stage of capitalism'), published in early July, Lenin noted that the Treaty of Versailles demonstrated that raw economics underlay the international policies of the Allied powers. His *Theses* (which some could see as rivalling Woodrow Wilson's Fourteen Points; see panel, p. 50) mark an important change in his thinking. Revolution in the colonies, he was now ready to claim, need not await revolution in Europe if it could develop from tactical alliance with non-communist liberation movements. This claim aroused bitter controversy in the first days of the congress. A commission including Sneevliet, M N Roy, Lenin's ally Georgy

Safarov and others, and chaired by Lenin himself, had the task of hammering out a revised text of the relevant clause of the *Theses*. Safarov proposed Roy as vice-chairman, Roy politely counter-proposed Sneevliet, and (it seems) Sneevliet modestly suggested Safarov; Lenin quickly accepted this and asked Sneevliet to be secretary.

The truly contentious issue arose in Thesis 11: communists must ally themselves with 'bourgeois-democratic' liberation movements. Lenin reached this conclusion because in colonial territories communists were thin on the ground and unable to organise legally: only by infiltrating a more moderate grouping could they hope to become strong enough to launch a revolution. This host group was likely to be nationalist; communists must therefore be ready to work with nationalism and 'make concessions' (Thesis 12), admitting that this would temporarily conflict with their eventual aim of world unity. Sneevliet temperamentally favoured the strategy and indeed had always worked in this way. After discussion a few textual revisions were made: Lenin replaced the term 'bourgeois-democratic' with 'national-revolutionary', and added that the form of any support for such movements 'must be discussed with the Communist Party of the country in question if there is such a party'.[11] But Roy, who fundamentally opposed alliances with non-communist groups, pressed his opposition until his alternative text, alongside the revised version of Lenin's, had to be put to the full Congress.

> 'There is a need to work with revolutionary nationalist elements, and we are only doing half the job if we reject this movement and play at being doctrinaire Marxists.'
> HENK SNEEVLIET AT THE SECOND COMINTERN CONGRESS, JULY 1920

Lenin, Sneevliet and Roy all spoke in the plenary debate on the subject. In theory, Lenin admitted, 'with the aid of the

LENIN'S DRAFT THESES ON NATIONAL AND COLONIAL QUESTIONS, 5 JUNE 1920
In submitting this draft for discussion by the Second Congress of the Communist International I ask all comrades, especially those with concrete information on these complex problems, to let me have their comments, amendments and additions in concise form ...

N. Lenin
5 June 1920

DRAFT THESES ON NATIONAL AND COLONIAL QUESTIONS

1.... Under the guise of individual equality, bourgeois democracy proclaims the formal equality of the property-owner and the proletarian, the exploiter and the exploited, thereby deceiving the oppressed classes ...

2.... The Communist Party must base its policy ... first, on an appraisal of the historical situation and of economic conditions; second, on a distinction between national interests as a general concept and the interests of oppressed classes ...; third, on a distinction between the oppressed, dependent and subject nations and the oppressing, exploiting and sovereign nations, so as to make evident ... the enslavement of the vast majority of the world's population by a small minority of ... capitalist countries, a feature characteristic of the era of finance capital and imperialism.

3.... The Western democracies' Treaty of Versailles is a fouler act of violence against weak nations than was the Treaty of Brest-Litovsk ... The League of Nations and the postwar policy of the Entente reveal this ever more clearly. These conditions intensify the revolutionary struggle, both of the proletariat in advanced countries and of the working masses in colonial and dependent countries, hastening the collapse of the ... illusion that nations can live together in peace and equality under capitalism.

4.... It follows that the Comintern's policy on national and colonial questions should rest on a union of proletarians and working masses ... for a joint revolutionary struggle to overthrow the landowners and the bourgeoisie ...

5. The world political situation has put dictatorship of the proletariat on the agenda ... The focus is the struggle of the world bourgeoisie against the Soviet Russian Republic, around which are grouped the Soviet movements of advanced workers in all countries and national liberation movements in the colonies and among oppressed nationalities ...

6.... . A policy must be pursued that will achieve alliance with Soviet Russia of all national and colonial liberation movements, its form determined by the degree of development of the communist movement in each country and of the bourgeois-democratic liberation movement of workers and peasants among backward nationalities.

7. Federation is a transition to the complete unity of working people of different nations. Its feasibility has been demonstrated by the relations between the R.S.F.S.R. and other Soviet Republics ... and nationalities which formerly enjoyed no autonomy ...

8. It is the Comintern's task to ... test these new federations arising on the basis of the Soviet system ... and to strive for ever closer unity, bearing in mind that the Soviet republics ... cannot possibly continue to exist ..., the productive forces ruined by imperialism cannot be restored, and the well-being of working people cannot be ensured without the closest alliance; also that there is a tendency towards the creation of a single world economy regulated by the proletariat of all nations as an integral whole and according to a common plan ...

9. National policy ... must go beyond the formal ... recognition of the equality of nations that is accorded by bourgeois democrats (... including socialists of the Second International)... . Communist parties must expose capitalist countries' violations of the equality of nations and of minority rights ..., must insist that only the Soviet system can ensure equality of nations ..., and must aid revolutionary movements among dependent and underprivileged nations (Ireland, American Negroes, etc.) and in the colonies ...

10.... . In countries that are already fully capitalist and have workers' parties that really act as the vanguard of the proletariat, the struggle against opportunist and petty-bourgeois pacifist distortions of the concept of internationalism is a primary task.

11. In backward nations in which feudal or patriarchal and patriarchal-peasant relations predominate, we must bear in mind:

first, the duty of Communist parties to assist the bourgeois-democratic liberation movement and the obligation of workers of the country on which the backward nation is dependent to give active assistance;

second, the need for struggle against religious, reactionary and medieval elements ..., Pan-Islamism and similar trends that attempt to use the liberation movement ... to strengthen the position of khans, landowners, mullahs, etc.;

third, the need ... to give the peasant movement against

landowners ... a revolutionary character by alliance with the West European communist proletariat ..., and to apply the basic principles of the Soviet system (by setting up working people's Soviets, etc.) in countries where pre-capitalist relations predominate;

fourth, the need to oppose attempts to give a communist colouring to bourgeois-democratic liberation trends in backward countries. The Comintern should support bourgeois-democratic national movements in colonial and backward countries only with the assurance that the elements of future proletarian and truly communist parties are being brought together and trained in the struggle against bourgeois-democratic movements. The Comintern must enter into a temporary alliance with bourgeois democracy in colonial and backward countries, but not merge with it, and should uphold the independence of the proletarian movement even if in embryonic form;

fifth, the need to explain to the working masses of all countries, particularly the backward countries, the deception practised by imperialist powers in setting up, under the guise of independence, states that are dependent economically, financially and militarily ... There is no salvation for dependent and weak nations except in a union of Soviet republics.

12. Oppression ... by imperialism has filled the working masses in oppressed countries with hatred towards oppressor nations; it has aroused distrust in these nations in general and even in their proletariat. The betrayal of socialism by ... official proletariat leaders in 1914–19, in using 'defence of country' to ... cloak their 'own' bourgeoisie's 'right' to oppress colonies and fleece financially dependent countries, increased this distrust. The more backward the country, the stronger is the hold of small-scale agriculture, patriarchalism and isolation: these lend strength and tenacity to petty-bourgeois prejudice, to national egoism and narrow-mindedness. These ... can disappear only when imperialism and capitalism have disappeared and the ... foundation of economic life has changed. The class-conscious communist proletariat of all countries must be conscious of survivals of national sentiments among long-oppressed nationalities and must make concessions so as to overcome distrust and prejudice more rapidly. Victory over capitalism cannot be won unless the proletariat and the mass of working people ... throughout the world strive for alliance and unity.[10]

proletariat of the advanced countries, backward countries can [advance] to communism without having to pass through the capitalist stage'. When it came to practice, however, 'it would be utopian to think that proletarian parties, if they manage to arise at all in these countries, will be able to carry out Communist tactics ... without having a definite relationship with the peasant movement, without supporting it in action'. Sneevliet, for his part, attempted to goad his fellow-delegates into engagement with the colonial question: 'There is no single question on the agenda that is as important in advancing the world revolution!' He insisted that the difficulty of 'finding the correct approach to relations between revolutionary-nationalist and socialist movements' was one of words: 'In practice this difficulty does not exist. We have to work with revolutionary-nationalist elements, and we are doing only half the job if we reject that movement and pose as doctrinaire Marxists.' But in stating his impression 'that with a few exceptions even this Congress ... has not fully understood the significance of the Oriental question',[12] he was unfortunately right; bored with the topic, the Congress inconsistently approved Roy's text as well as Lenin's *Theses*. It was the latter, however, that made policy for the next several years, and it would be for Sneevliet and others to attempt to apply it.

At the same Congress Lenin took up the idea of a training school in Russia for potential revolutionary leaders. Moscow was the 'new Mecca', Sneevliet urged; Russia must make available 'a theoretical education in Communism ... so as to help make the Far East an active member of the Communist International'.[13] This was to be the Communist University of the Workers of the East, founded in 1921 and later called the 'Stalin School'.

Back in Indonesia, the battle between Sarekat Islam and the

PKI came to a head towards the end of 1920. They had courted the support of labour unions and vied with one another for the privilege of supporting strikes, with very variable success. Now, on 20 October, Surjopranoto, a leader of the large sugar workers' union and (under the broad umbrella of Sarekat Islam) a bitter opponent of Semaun, had an interview with the Governor-General, van Limburg Stirum. Two days later – it can hardly have been a coincidence – the sugar workers announced their decision no longer to co-operate with the communists and their labour union wing. That this was a serious blow for the PKI is evident from the sequel. Anonymous articles in *Sinar Hindia*, the Indonesian newspaper of the communist leaders, wondered what deal had been struck at the meeting; then a signed article by Darsono followed, smearing Tjokroaminoto as an embezzler of Sarekat Islam funds. The accusation was never pursued (Darsono eventually withdrew it and apologised).[14] Tjokroaminoto had thus far laboured against all difficulties to hold Sarekat Islam together and to keep Semaun and the communists as part of it. He now decided that communists must be excluded from the organisation, and did his best to ensure that local Sarekat Islam shared his view. The following year Tjokroaminoto himself came under attack: he was arrested, to be held in prison for some months, unfairly accused of backing a secret and seditious group led by the radicals Alimin and Musso, disingenuously calling itself *Sarekat Islam afdeeling B (*Section B).

Sneevliet, meanwhile, had left Moscow and was bound for China, on Comintern instructions and at Lenin's personal suggestion, where he was to establish regular links with the Chinese Communist Party.[15] He was not allowed to disembark at British ports *en route* because of his police record. However, his journey east was made less irksome when he was joined at

Singapore by his friends Darsono and Asser Baars, on the first leg of the long journey to Russia, where Darsono was to attend the Third Comintern Congress.[16] The three arrived in Shanghai on 4 June 1921. After witnessing the official birth of the Chinese Communist Party at the First Congress in Shanghai in July (the young Mao Zedong participating), Sneevliet's next job was to organise a secretariat for the nascent communist labour movement and from this to assemble a Chinese delegation to go to Moscow for the First Congress of the Workers of the East. Semaun, who met his old mentor in Shanghai before travelling onwards, was to go with them.

Semaun, now aged twenty-two, had travelled further than any other delegate. He spoke little or no Russian but presented a report in the form of a rapid history of the Indonesian nationalist movement and of the tiny Communist Party that had set out to work within it, just as Lenin's *Theses* now instructed. It hardly seemed to matter that this strategy had collapsed; Semaun made a powerful impression on the Congress and also attracted Lenin's personal interest. In a long conversation Lenin urged him to continue working in alliance with non-communist groups and not to rush into revolution. Asian communist parties faced their own challenges:

Alimin (Mas Alimin Prawirodirdjo) (1889–?) was a well-educated union activist, involved in Sarekat Islam 'Afdeeling B', then PKI. He urged Comintern backing for the 1926 uprising. He led the PKI after 1948 but was sidelined by 1953. He wrote *Riwajat hidup* ('Autobiography' in 1954).

Musso or Moeso (1897–1948) was involved in Sarekat Islam 'Afdeeling B', then PKI. He urged Comintern backing for 1926 uprising, set up 'Illegal PKI' in 1935, then retreated to Moscow. He returned, led an uprising in 1948 and was killed.

Tan Malaka (*c.* 1897–1949) studied in the Netherlands. He was chairman of PKI in 1921; expelled from Dutch Indies 1922; he attended Fourth Comintern Congress in 1922 and worked for Comintern in South East Asia from 1923. He returned to Indonesia in 1942.

they should not expect that adopting Russian tactics would allow them to replicate the Russian revolution.

In preparation for his voyage to Russia, Semaun had resigned the chair of the PKI. Darsono, popular enough to have claimed the succession, was still out of the country. At its congress at Semarang in December 1921 the party elected as chairman Tan Malaka, aged about twenty-four, son of a village headman in Minangkabau (west Sumatra) who had started a series of self-financing schools which were helping to spread Marxist ideas. Having taken control, he almost immediately began agitation in favour of a general strike. Dirk Fock, who had replaced Van Limburg Stirum as Governor-General, with strong direction from a newly conservative Dutch government and quite unexpected speed, condemned Tan Malaka to exile. He had led the party for just three months.

As a result Semaun returned in May 1922 to find the labour movement and the PKI demoralised. Re-assuming the vacant chairmanship, Semaun urged the need for propaganda and proselytising, and had some initial success. Meanwhile, after the experience of 1920 and 1921, Tjokroaminoto was at last convinced that Sarekat Islam needed party unity and discipline, and at a congress at Madiun in February 1923 he brought most of the old association into a new *Partai Sarekat Islam* from which members of the PKI were excluded. He also continued to speak, more clearly than any of the others, for unity, including the unity of the many peoples of the Indies. Thus, while urging autonomy and eventual independence, he explicitly opposed narrow nationalism such as Darsono had espoused: 'Let us make no distinction between races and peoples, Sumatrans, Balinese, Javanese and peoples from Sulawesi and Borneo, for they are all Indiërs [Indonesians].' [17]

This upheaval left the PKI isolated and significantly weaker.

Government staff cuts having now been followed by wage cuts, there were powerful calls for strikes among civil servants and rail workers. Semaun and Darsono foresaw failure and tried to discourage action. But between disaffected and powerless workers and a suddenly determined administration there was no room for communist leaders, however conciliatory. More than 100 activists were detained, Semaun and

> 'Let us make no distinction between races and peoples, Sumatrans, Balinese, Javanese and peoples from Sulawesi and Borneo, for they are all Indiërs.'
>
> **TJOKROAMINOTO, FEBRUARY 1923**

Darsono among them. Semaun's arrest (on dubious evidence) provoked a railway strike, against which the administration acted harshly, claiming disingenuously that 'a strike occurring as a reaction to the application of the general legal code undoubtedly has a revolutionary character. All leading figures in the [rail union] are equally guilty. None of them have spoken against the calling of a strike.' [18] There is room for suspicion that Governor-General Fock intentionally provoked the showdown. In August 1923 Semaun was exiled to the Netherlands, where he became the PKI's representative to the Dutch Communist Party; almost at the same moment, Henk Sneevliet, after two years of work in China for the Comintern, returned to the Netherlands and immersed himself in communist and union affairs.

Six months earlier Tan Malaka had departed for the same destination; he then made his way, in November 1922, to Moscow to represent the Dutch Indies at the Fourth Comintern Congress, where, though Lenin was now ill and losing his grip on events, the policy of alliance was still favoured (the break-up of the PKI's alliance with Sarekat Islam passed unremarked). After nearly a year in Moscow, Tan Malaka was chosen to represent the Comintern in the Far East and was ordered to Guangzhou (Canton). His instructions were to guide the policies of the PKI from outside the borders of the Dutch Indies. From Moscow's perspective the need for this was clear: a communist party must follow Comintern decisions, yet communist activists inside the country, especially if in touch with Moscow, risked immediate arrest and exile. It was an impossible assignment.

At its June 1924 congress, with Darsono surviving and Alimin and Musso emerging as leading lights, the PKI definitively renamed itself *Partai Komunis Indonesia*; Indonesia, as a name for the lands currently ruled as the Dutch Indies, was now gaining currency. The party's numbers had slowly increased, though even at their height – and including members of affiliated unions – it counted fewer than 50,000 sympathisers. It is astonishing, then, that at a special congress in December at Kutagede, near Yogyakarta, the Party quietly took the decision to mount a revolution. Semaun in the Netherlands and Tan Malaka in Guangzhou were taken aback by this. Malaka fiercely opposed it, in accord with Comintern policy and with the advice that a succession of Indies communists had received from Lenin: revolutions that were unlikely to succeed were not to be undertaken. The Comintern sternly ordered the PKI to remake its alliance with Sarekat Islam, and in early 1925 the party made belated attempts to do this, with limited enthusiasm and no success. Malaka put forward his own views in his essay *Naar de 'Republiek Indonesia'* ('Towards the "Republic of Indonesia"') published in Guangzhou: he spoke for the 'immediate provision of the full right to vote to the Indonesian people, both male and female', for 'acknowledgement of religious freedom' and other human rights, for nationalisation, but not for revolution.[19]

Tan Malaka now shifted to the Philippines, where he made

contact with the communist labour leader Crisanto Evangelista as well as mainstream politicians like Manuel Quezon. Even there, slightly closer to his homeland, communication was slow and uncertain and the influence he could wield was negligible. The PKI's planned revolution was no secret; the colonial administration watched known activists keenly, and encouraged the anti-communist vigilante groups that during 1925 went on the attack in many districts (disrupting Tan Malaka's schools among other targets). In response, the PKI resolved to increase its own agitation in the countryside, in preparation for imminent liberation, and to make contact with the unorganised 'bandits' who – in this as in other South East Asian countries – disturbed colonial peace. Impatient for revolution, communist unions started strikes in July 1925. There were many arrests; Alimin fled to join Tan Malaka in Manila; Darsono was exiled; a group of activists gathered in Singapore, from where Alimin and Musso set out for Moscow to get Comintern backing.

The two Indonesians spoke before the Comintern executive committee in June 1926, joined by Semaun, who travelled from Amsterdam, and Darsono, already in Moscow. If we can trust French intelligence reports, Semaun brought to this meeting news of communist stirrings in the Chinese communities of Burma, Siam, Indochina and Malaya, as well as the Dutch Indies.[20] A second meeting took place three months later, and this time the all-powerful Stalin was present. But Russia was at that moment more interested in relations with European colonialists than with oppressed peoples of the colonies. The reply to Alimin and Musso was that it was not yet time for revolution in the Dutch Indies and there would be no significant support. Alimin and Musso made their way slowly home, and were arrested in Johor on 18 December, with $2,500 in American currency.[21]

In the Dutch Indies, however, desultory local preparations had continued. The outcome would put back the cause of self-determination for many years to come. The revolution in Java, such as it was, happened in November 1926. Local administrators intercepted the crucial messages and put down the uprising almost before it began. In Minangkabau there were a few days of fighting in January 1927 and some deaths. The only real results were the mass arrest of 13,000 communist activists and sympathisers, some executions, 500 prison sentences and 1,308 deportations to prison camps in Dutch New Guinea. Political resistance to colonial rule would scarcely revive before the Japanese invasion.

5

Demands of the Vietnamese People, 1906–26

The Vietnamese 'Claims', in the *Revendications du peuple annamite* presented in Paris in 1919, were to be frustrated at the Peace Conference, which did not discuss the points raised, let alone make any moves towards self-determination for French Indochina. Resistance to French rule in Indochina had, however, been a long time coming. Of the three Vietnamese linked with the *Revendications,* the first to come to official notice had been Phan Chu Trinh. At the age of 13, in 1885, Trinh and his father, subjects of Annam, fought for the Emperor Hàm Nghi in his ill-fated rebellion against French overlordship. Trinh's father was killed by fellow rebels, Hàm Nghi was eventually captured, deposed and exiled to Algeria, and Trinh returned home to find his house burned down and his family destitute. Ever since these horrific events he had followed his own path. A critical student of the old Chinese learning, he briefly served the Ministry of Rites at Huế; but by 1906 he was ready to speak out. Dedicated to peace, he had become utterly disillusioned with the downtrodden position of Annam under its threefold burden: a native civil service steeped in ancient

French acquisitions in South East Asia took place in several steps. Cochinchine, the southern region surrounding Saigon, was conquered in 1859–62; the Vietnamese empire retained Annam, the narrow central strip of Vietnam with its capital at Huế. But in 1874 Annam became a French protectorate, nominally ruled by the Emperor but under strict French control. Tonkin, with its capital Hanoi, once the heartland of imperial Vietnam, was unsuccessfully invaded in 1873, then conquered in the Sino-French War of 1884–5. In 1887 these three territories (which now comprise modern Vietnam) were united as 'French Indochina', the responsibility of a French Governor-General eventually based at Hanoi. To them were added the kingdom of Cambodia, which had invited French protection in 1863 (an arrangement recognised by Siam in 1867), and the three principalities of Laos (Luang Prabang, Vientiane and Champasak), formerly subject to Siam. France assumed a protectorate over these in 1893.

learning, a godlike puppet emperor and an irresistible French 'protectorate'. The old-established colony of Cochinchine was peaceful; the northern territory of Tonkin was still intermittently disturbed by warlords and 'pirates', heirs of the Pavillons Noirs who had opposed the French invasion.

The frankness of the long open letter that he addressed in August 1906 to the Governor-General of Indochina might well, in almost any other year, have led to his arrest as a troublemaker; or it might just have been ignored. But Governor-General Paul Beau had the letter translated and published it in full, without adverse comment, in the official section of the *Bulletin de l'Ecole Française d'Extrême-Orient* – the scholarly journal of French Far Eastern research and exploration. 'Since Annam was placed under their protectorate the French have installed roads, bridges, navigable waterways, railways, postal services and telegraphs, and no one will dispute the obvious benefits of these developments,' wrote Phan Chu Trinh. 'But they have given no attention to administrative abuses, nor to the rapid advance of destitution and moral decline among the people, and it is in this that they are to be condemned; they have closed their eyes to these evils that overwhelm our nation and are destroying it.' He added detailed criticism of the excessive freedom allowed to the old imperial civil service with its traditionally-educated, long-haired employees; of French mistrust of the Annamese, and of the complete separation between the two. 'The French authorities, having no links with us, sharing no common interests with us, are ignorant of all this … The weight of taxes crushes rich and poor alike. The roads are crowded with bands of starving people; theft and brigandage are everywhere; waves of hatred rise like a menacing tide … It is a near certainty that if France were at war with a foreign power and were not immediately victorious, the mass of people would take advantage of this to rebel: the foam would rise to the surface.'

> 'It is a near certainty that if France were at war with a foreign power and were not immediately victorious, the mass of people would take advantage of this to rebel.'
>
> **PHAN CHU TRINH, 1906**

Thus he urged the Governor-General to remove the oppressively learned local administrators.[1] Paul Beau's mission since his appointment in 1902 had been to break with the expansionist past. The policy was now to develop the colony within its existing borders and to enhance the welfare of its people. His response to Phan Chu Trinh in 1906 was in line with this policy. There was another impulse in play too. About a year earlier – very soon after the Japanese victory in the Russo-Japanese War – the colonial *Sûreté* had become aware of a serious new threat posed by a self-exiled anti-colonialist, Phan Bội Châu, who had established himself in Japan and was encouraging young Vietnamese to travel east (this was the *Đông Du* or 'go east' movement) in order to study in the one Asiatic country that had demonstrated its ability to defeat the Europeans. Several hotels and businesses had turned out to be fronts for channelling students and money to Japan and distributing Phan Bội Châu's writings, his *History of the Loss of Vietnam* and his haunting poem *Book Written in Blood in a Foreign Land*.[2] Meanwhile the most adventurous member of the Annamese imperial family, Prince Cường Để, regarded by the French administration until this point as a possible substitute if it became necessary to depose the current emperor Thành Thái, silently disappeared from Huế in January 1906. He travelled incognito to Hong Kong; Phan Bội Châu came there to meet him and they returned to Japan together. This dangerously subversive trend had to be countered, and the anti-royalist and anti-civil servant Phan Chu Trinh was – temporarily – seen as a safe alternative voice.

It must have been for similar reasons that permission was given to open the *Đông Kinh Nghĩa Thục*, the Eastern Capital Free School, in Hanoi. Here students of all ages were able to take classes in science, philosophy, Vietnamese and Western literature; Phan Chu Trinh was a popular teacher there. It could not last. Police investigations found subversive texts being distributed and innocuous-seeming businesses secretly gathering money for rebel groups, and after just a few months, in November 1907, the school was shut down. Searches showed that it, too, had been directing students to Phan Bội Châu.[3] Late the same year, in one of his last acts before he left for France in February 1908, Paul Beau hastily put together a plan for a colonial-style University of Hanoi instead: 'This initiative will surely have its effect in indigenous circles,' he reported to Paris, 'among whom Chinese and Japanese universities enjoy prestige and power of attraction: some students have already been making the journey to Japan.'[4]

Beau's successors, Louis Bonhoure and Antony Klobu-kowski, dealt severely with the difficult aftermath of the liberal Beau years. There were widespread demonstrations against taxation and oppressive administration. Badly-behaved young men went around with scissors, cutting the traditionalists' long hair and singing 'Cut out ignorance! End stupidity! Snip! Snip!', a song popularised by the short-lived Free School. The protests were put down violently, and although Phan Chu Trinh had taken no part, he was arrested and sent home to be tried for sedition, a capital offence, under the harsh judicial system of his native Annam. Only on the plea of the Paris Human Rights League was his sentence commuted to life imprisonment on the prison island Côn Sơn. It was now that Nguyễn Tất Thành (Hồ Chí Minh), aged seventeen, son of a minor administrator and admirer of Phan Bội Châu, had his first experience of colonial politics. He stepped forward to interpret between a delegation of villagers and their rulers, was badly beaten, and on the following day was traced to his school by the police and expelled at their insistence.[5]

A month later, on the night of 27 June 1908, acting Governor-General Louis Bonhoure learned to his horror that the French garrison at Hanoi, 200-strong, had been poisoned at an official banquet using the hallucinogen *Datura metel*. An antidote was adminstered and no one died but official reaction was swift and severe, no doubt influenced by the French settlers in Hanoi who, suddenly aware of their vulnerability, had demonstrated in front of the governor's residence. Courts were suspended, to be replaced by those Special Tribunals of which, eleven years later, Hồ Chí Minh, the Indochina delegate in Paris, was to complain. There were at least twenty public beheadings and many lengthy prison terms were handed out.[6]

A lasting consequence was the final abandonment of the

liberal policy identified with Paul Beau. One of Klobukowski's first acts was a symbolic one: he closed the still-embryonic University of Hanoi. Another was to put pressure on the Japanese government to end its tolerance of the activities of Phan Bội Châu, which were shown to menace the security of French Indochina. Eventually succumbing, the Japanese authorities expelled him on 8 March 1909. Intense diplomatic pressure was also exerted over Prince Cường Để. He went to ground for several months, until, in October 1909, the Japanese police could no longer keep up the pretence of being unable to find him and he was put on board ship for Shanghai. The once-thriving band of Vietnamese students in Japan was left leaderless and almost without resources. Soon few remained.

Both Cường Để and Phan Bội Châu eventually made their way to Siam. In the north-east of the country, within reach of the Mekong and the Indochina border, communities of Vietnamese refugees and émigrés lived and prospered under the benevolent eye of the monarchy. Back in 1908 Châu had gained support for his anti-French activities from King Chulalongkorn but his successor, the young and changeable Vajiravudh, was less enthusiastic. Settlement in Siam was permitted but the use of Siam as a base for action against French Indochina was not. Southern China was more hospitable, under the aegis of the newly powerful Sun Yatsen and his *Tongmenghui* or Chinese Unification Society (forerunner of the *Guomindang*). Here, a sort of Vietnamese government-in-exile, the *Việt Nam Quang Phục Hội* or Vietnam Restoration Society, was established in June 1912 with Cường Để as president.

On its instructions two attempted assassinations were launched: an attack on the new French Governor-General, Albert Sarraut, in November 1912, which was a fiasco, and the bomb that killed two French officers at a café in Hanoi in April

1913. This was a Pyrrhic victory: there followed another Special Tribunal, seven beheadings and 57 gaol sentences. There were death sentences *in absentia* for Châu and Cường Để.[8] It is astonishing to realise that at this very time the Prince was in hiding in Cochinchine. In an act of remarkable bravery, he had stowed away among the cabin boys on a French steamer bound for Saigon, and for three months travelled incognito around the province. Many recognised him and no one betrayed him; only on his return to Hong Kong was he briefly imprisoned. He paid his way out of gaol and travelled to Europe.

Appointed Governor-General under a radical French government, Albert Sarraut's first duty was to apply new legislation of 20 October 1911 that made concessions on local government to French Indochina. He was to hold the post twice, ruling the colony until May 1919. He argued for *association* between colonialists and their colonies, but he had in mind an unequal relationship, as of foster-parent with foster-child, and he was fated to be snubbed by Vietnamese, who on occasion made it clear to him that they wanted no such relationship.

Cường Để responded to Sarraut's new approach in 1913, writing from London to offer co-operation, but set various conditions, among them a ban on opium (socially destructive, but an economic mainstay of colonial administrations in Asia)

Sun Yatsen (Sun Yixian) (1866–1925) was born in southern China; educated in American-occupied Hawaii, he was technically an American citizen. He was active politically from 1894, often in exile; he led a coalition whose aim was to establish democracy in China. He became provisional president of China, January-April 1912, and founded the Guomindang in August 1912. Sun ruled southern China from 1921 and co-operated with the Communists. In Japan in 1905 Sun formulated his Three Principles of the People: Minzu, Minquan, Minsheng, which might be roughly translated, with a nod to the Gettysburg Address that may have inspired them, as 'Government of the people, by the people, for the people'.[7]

and the reprieve of all political prisoners and exiles. Sarraut turned him down, and in 1915 the Prince found safe refuge once again in Japan, which was able to resist French pressure now that France was preoccupied with the European War. The war, in fact, was Japan's opportunity to advance its regional position. In its Twenty-One Demands to China, in 1915, Japan assumed the dominance that such colonial powers as Germany had previously wielded. The same approach, a threat to China, was a promise to the Vietnamese. 'No one can predict how the European war will turn out,' a government minister advised Cường Để in 1916. 'If France loses, Japan will help Vietnam to gain its freedom; it will not allow Vietnam to slip from French hands into those of others.'[9]

Indochina, like other colonial territories in South East Asia, suffered severely from the economic distortions of the First World War. There was a series of uprisings. Cường Để's continuing exile made him a useful scapegoat for a rebellion in Cochinchine in February 1916 (after which, as after the poisoning plot, demonstrations by French settlers were followed by a Special Tribunal and public beheadings). Three months later the Emperor Duy Tân, now sixteen, and his learned adviser Trần Cao Vân, attempted an uprising in Huế. Vân had been among those imprisoned at Côn Sơn after the tax protests in 1908. This time, on capture, he was executed. Duy Tân, along with his errant father Thành Thái, was exiled to the Indian Ocean island of Réunion, the third successive Emperor of Annam to have been deposed under French suzerainty.

Phan Chu Trinh, benefiting once more from the distant tutelage of the Human Rights League, had been unexpectedly released from Côn Sơn in early 1911 and dispatched to Paris, initially granted a French government stipend, though if this was intended to silence him, it failed. In an article for the League's *Bulletin* he recalled the killings that followed the tax demonstrations of 1908. 'Remember that it was the French colonial authorities that killed your father,' he imagined a mother telling her children. 'Never forget that when you grow up you also may have the same fate.' [10] Soon after the beginning of the First World War he and his lawyer friend Phan Văn Trường came under suspicion of conspiring with the Germans. Each spent nearly a year in prison.

Hồ Chí Minh had left Indochina two months after Phan Chu Trinh's departure. 'The people of Vietnam, including my own father, often wondered who would help them to remove the yoke of French control,' he told an interviewer long afterwards. 'Some said Japan, others Great Britain, and some said the United States. I saw that I must go abroad to see for myself.' [11] The list was no fantasy. Japan had just defeated Russia; the United States had seized the Philippines from Spain and had promised eventual independence; Britain was France's great rival in South East Asia. Hồ had kept out of the way of the authorities for three years, latterly taking refuge in the anonymity of Saigon where he had made a little money selling medicinal herbs. In June 1911, he took a job as galley assistant aboard the *Amiral Latouche-Tréville*. By September he was in Marseille, and boldly sent an application to the French President for admission to the prestigious Ecole Coloniale – which was open not only to future French administrators, but also to natives of the French colonies who acted as teaching assistants. 'I would wish to become useful to France in relation to

'The people of Vietnam often wondered who would help them to remove the yoke of French control. Some said Japan, others Great Britain, and some said the United States. I saw that I must go abroad to see for myself.'

HỒ CHÍ MINH TO ANNA LOUISE STRONG, C. 1963

my compatriots, and at the same time to enable them to profit from the advantages of instruction,' he wrote.[12] Admissions were subject to political approval, the résident supérieur at Huế advised against him, and his application failed.[13] Hồ spent two years at sea, and at least four years in London, surviving thanks to low-paid work in kitchens and hotels, before arriving in Paris at some unknown date between 1917 and early 1919. He was, as we know, certainly present in the French capital during the closing weeks of the Peace Conference.

In Japan, meanwhile, Prince Cường Để was not inactive. The Paris Peace Conference had opened in January 1919; a year earlier President Wilson had highlighted in his Fourteen Points the need to take the wishes of the inhabitants into account when deciding territorial claims. On 12 February 1919, the Prince, as president of the Vietnam Restoration Society, dispatched a telegram to Albert Sarraut in Hanoi: 'The Annamese are highly dissatisfied under the present form of government and much desire to be granted immediate liberty.' A second telegram went to President Wilson in Paris. Thanks to him, the Prince wrote, Germany had been defeated and peace proclaimed. The Vietnamese requested immediate assistance from the United States to free their country from its present colonial government; they also requested admission to the League of Nations. In addition, inspired by Wilson's Fourteen Points, he addressed an open letter to the Peace Conference: 'France is the elder sister of republican governments and the champion of civilisation. Their rule of Vietnam by right of conquest is barbaric and contrary to principle … We ask you to return our independence, our freedom, our rights and our country and to permit us to live in liberty at last.' [14] France responded to these moves with immediate diplomatic pressure on Japan, making pointed reference to the expulsions of 1909; but, conveniently, the Prince had made a short trip to China to confer with Phan Bội Châu (recently freed from gaol there). Japan was therefore able to reply that Cường Để was not in the country at all. After further reflection, in March 1919 Albert Sarraut decided instead to encourage Japan to continue to accommodate the Prince; it was better for him to stay there than wander the world untraceably. This was one of Sarraut's last acts as Governor-General of Indochina. He left for Paris in May, there to take office as Colonial Minister and to make the acquaintance of Hồ Chí Minh.

At the Congress at Tours in December 1920 Hồ Chí Minh denounced conditions in Vietnam and demanded that the 'Socialist Party must act effectively in favour of oppressed native peoples'. Now a founder member of the French Communist Party, he worked on in Paris for more than two years. He led his small Vietnamese group into the newly-formed anti-colonial pressure group Action Coloniale, and edited its monthly paper, Le paria. He went on writing for L'humanité on the cruelties and privations of colonial Indochina. He attended meetings assiduously. But it was becoming obvious, to him and to his old mentor, that there was much more to do and that only he could do it. 'I see myself as an exhausted horse who can no longer gallop,' Phan Chu Trinh wrote to him in a long letter of fatherly advice; 'I want to compare you to a fiery stallion ... I hope you will listen to me as you prepare your grand design.'[15] Trinh himself at this moment was in Marseille, developing a publicity campaign against the puppet emperor Khải Định's much-heralded visit to the forthcoming Colonial Exhibition. Hồ joined this campaign with a long-forgotten satirical play, Le dragon de bambou. All this was no more than a sideshow, however, as they both knew. Trinh pressed Hồ to return to Vietnam; a born teacher himself, he saw Hồ in the same light, and he knew that political meetings and small-circulation papers in foreign cities would never change minds in Vietnam. Hồ agreed,[16] but he was to re-enter Vietnam in his own time and by his own route.

The new Governor-General of Indochina, the career colonialist Martial Merlin, telegraphed Sarraut on 2 November 1923 to urge an ever-closer watch on the Vietnamese in Paris. 'Refuse or confiscate passports Phan-châu-Trinh, Phan-van-Truong, Nguyên-ai-Quôc.' It was to no avail. The Indochina delegate's departure from Paris was as unobtrusive as his arrival. In June 1923 Hồ Chí Minh left Paris for a one-week holiday in Savoie, taking none of his few possessions and saying nothing to his friends or to colleagues at *Le paria*. He never arrived in Savoie and (as the minister was compelled to admit in his reply to Martial Merlin) eventually proved to have had a quite different destination: 'Your recommendations noted. Nguyên-ai-Quôc return from Moscow awaited momentarily, where he went without passport ... Regret unable refuse passport Phan-van-Truong, French citizen, barrister. Would provoke noisy opposition Human Rights League and probably questions Parliament.'[17] Hồ was indeed in Moscow, where clearly his purpose was to get Comintern backing to develop a communist revolutionary movement in Indochina by way of southern China. China was the choice because of all Indochina's land neighbours China was the least unfriendly to revolution; also because Vietnamese could operate unobtrusively there, as Phan Bội Châu had demonstrated.

Hồ's immediate priority was to arouse interest and gain sympathy. Moscow had heard very little about Indochina and much about the Dutch Indies. On arrival he was invited to make a report to the Comintern's Indonesia Commission (because there was no body with a more appropriate remit). Hồ's report was blunt. Lenin's *Theses* had aroused hopes of liberation in the colonies, he said. Colonial administrations had increased their propaganda and tightened their oppression; communist parties in Britain and France had expressed sympathy but done nothing.

He had arrived at a difficult time. Lenin had suffered a series of strokes and no longer took an active role. There was a power struggle, which Trotsky was losing and Stalin was winning; that was obvious to all, but it was not obvious in what form Lenin's policies on world communism, and on revolution in the colonies, would survive the upheaval. Meanwhile no one cared to decide whether, and under what terms, Hô should go to China. He waited; he wrote *Le procès de la colonisation française* ('French colonialism on trial'); he possibly studied at the Communist University of the Workers of the East;[18] he attended Lenin's funeral in January 1924 and came away with frostbitten hands and nose; and he attended the fifth Comintern Congress in June, where Grigory Zinoviev (at that time an ally of Stalin) painted an uncomfortable picture of Lenin's 'United Front' policy of alliance with, or infiltration of, non-Communist nationalist groups. Zinoviev referred to it as 'the most debated question in our ranks'. 'The tactic of the United Front remains correct', Zinoviev insisted, yet its origins were in defeatism, betraying 'the realisation that we have not yet won a majority of the working class … that we are on the defensive … and that the decisive struggle is not yet on the agenda.'[19] Semaun, exiled from the Dutch Indies, and M N Roy, now representing the Communist Party of India, were among the delegates at this fifth Congress, but it was the newcomer, Hô Chí Minh, who spoke out once more against the inactivity of European communist parties on colonial issues: 'All that our parties have done in this domain is equal to zero … In

Indochina the colonial powers have become slave-traders …
they are handing over a large portion of the colony to a consortium of sharks.' [20]

'In Indochina the colonial
powers have become
slave-traders.'

HỒ CHÍ MINH, 1924

Having achieved his aim in Moscow, Hồ arrived in Guangzhou (Canton) in November 1924; he was using a new name, Lý Thụy. He found that Henk Sneevliet had successfully implemented the Leninist United Front policy by cajoling, or rather coercing, the Chinese Communists into joining the *Guomindang* or Nationalist Party, led by Sun Yatsen, seconded by Liu Zhongkai, and now wielding power in Guangzhou.

Hồ's instructions were to work with the *Guomindang* and, as cover, to take a post with the Russian Telegraphic Agency.[21] But his real focus was to be on the Vietnamese. Since the old exile figureheads, Phan Bội Châu and Prince Cường Để, had gained nothing from their long flirtation with Japan, even their more faithful followers must be restless and open to offers from Moscow. Some younger emigrés had set up a new group, *Tâm Tâm Xã* (Like Minds Society); others were becoming students at the Guomindang's newly-established Huangpu (Whampoa) Military Academy, partly staffed by Russian advisers. Tâm Tâm Xã's proudest exploit had been carried out, in June 1924, independently of Châu. Governor-General Martial Merlin, guest of honour at a reception in the French concession of Shamian in Guangzhou harbour, had been targeted by a suitcase bomb. Merlin escaped unhurt, but three French guests were killed and many injured. The bomber, Phạm Hồng Thái, unable to evade the guards on the only bridge that linked the French enclave to the mainland, fell into the wide Zhu Jiang, drowned, and became a hero.

Nguyễn Hải Thần, one of the first students welcomed by

Châu to Japan in 1905, now his closest collaborator and heir apparent, seemed ready to work with Hồ. Châu himself wrote encouragingly: like Phan Chu Trinh, it seems, he saw Hồ as the man to take the work into a new generation, and, for all the difference in ideology, Hồ set to work in Phan's way, making contact with groups in Vietnam that would send him young men to train in his own makeshift propaganda school, or at the Huangpu Academy close at hand, or to send on to Russia. In accordance with Comintern instructions, he kept up links with the Philippines, with the Dutch Indies and with India. Ever the journalist, he began a news-sheet, *Thanh Niên* ('Youth'). He also helped to set up an international group bringing together revolutionaries from India, Korea, Vietnam and the Dutch Indies, who regarded Guangzhou as their local base, their eastern Moscow: this was the *Ligue des Peuples Opprimés* (League of Oppressed Peoples), first of a series of similarly-named organisations.[22] Its chairman, Liu Zhongkai, still the mainstay of the communist-Guomindang alliance, was to be assassinated just two months later.

> **Nguyễn Hải Thần** (c. 1878–1955) studied in Japan with Phan Bội Châu and worked closely with him in the early 1920s. He led Vietnamese nationalists in China in the 1930s, and collaborated uneasily with Hồ Chí Minh in 1925 and again after 1941. He was briefly vice-president in 1946; retired to China, where he died.

In Indochina in April 1925 Martial Merlin's term as Governor-General ended. Next month, the ageing Phan Chu Trinh arrived, permitted at last by the French government to return to his homeland. With him, returning from abandoned doctoral studies in Paris, came a much younger nationalist thinker and writer, Nguyễn An Ninh, whose father and aunt had provided refuges for Prince Cường Để during his secret visit to Indochina in 1913. Ninh himself had given a famous speech in October 1923, 'L'idéal de la jeunesse annamite' ('The ideals of young Vietnamese'), an unconscious echo of the theme chosen by May Oung in Burma in 1908.

Then in July 1925 Phan Bội Châu unwisely ventured from his retreat in southern China to the international territory of Shanghai and was arrested by the French police, tried in Hanoi and sentenced to death. Far more successful in captivity than he had ever been while free, he was the subject of massive and prolonged protest demonstrations in the cities of Indochina. The new leftist Governor-General Alexandre Varenne, to calm the protests and demonstrate his liberality, freed Châu in December to retire peacefully to Huế.

In truth Varenne brought little change to Indochina, as André Malraux, who had just arrived in Indochina, sharply predicted in his *L'Indochine enchaînée*. Malraux was a French citizen and could say pretty much what he liked, but on 24 March 1926 Nguyễn An Ninh was arrested, the first of many arrests, for having written in his magazine *La cloche fêlée* ('The cracked bell') in support of an imprisoned journalist. As a politician and intellectual, Ninh was to keep up the pressure for change in the French colony until the late 1930s. On the very day of Ninh's arrest, Phan Chu Trinh died in hospital in Saigon of the tuberculosis from which he had suffered for many years. He had lived for less than a year after his return. There were mass demonstrations of mourning lasting several days; some schoolchildren were expelled for wearing mourning bands.

Ironically, news of the trial of Phan Bội Châu taught some young Vietnamese for the first time that there was an active resistance movement based in southern China. Others who already knew of Hồ Chí Minh's presence there were expecting him to announce an uprising in 1926; but unlike his comrades in the Dutch Indies, Hồ never at this period supposed, or hinted, that revolution was imminent. He worked on, glad to be receiving more help and more recruits from Indochina. To him it did not at first matter that Sun Yatsen and Liu Zhongkai, allies of the Chinese communists, were both dead. He could ignore, at first, the ominous moves against communist infiltration in the Guomindang taken by the new strongman, Chiang Kai-shek, in March 1926. It was an irritation that Nguyễn Hải Thần, never a communist, was becoming an active rival; it was a worry that Moscow seemed to be losing interest in him. Hồ held on in Canton for another ever more precarious year, until a friend in the police told him to get out. Escaping by a few hours capture by the now anti-communist Guomindang, he fled to Hong Kong, Shanghai and Vladivostok. Nguyễn Hải Thần and the nationalists held on in China; Hồ Chí Minh would not return to Indochina until 1941.

Of all the colonialist participants in the 1919 Peace Conference, France was the least responsive to colonial pressure for self-determination. Partial independence, for southern Vietnam only, came at last in 1955. It would require another war with another colonial power – the United States – before real independence for the whole country was achieved.

6

Siam Reasserts Independence, 1917–39

In 1914, as the First World War began in Europe, it was not clear to King Vajiravudh of Siam whether it was in his country's interest to become involved. Germany was an occasional interloper in the South East Asian political scene and Austria was a distant irrelevance. So it was clear, at least, that alliance with them offered nothing. Worse, it could bring annihilation, because two enemies of Germany – Britain and France – were daily and dominant presences: all the territories that bordered Siam were ruled by one or other of these two. The choice lay, therefore, between neutrality (the correct choice if Germany were to win) and alliance with Britain and France.

There was little love for France, whose protectorate over Cambodia in 1863, takeover of Laos in 1893 and annexation of the remaining Cambodian provinces of Battambang and Siem-reap in 1907 had steadily deprived Siam of a vast swathe of its protective northern and eastern borderlands. The nightmare year of 1893, when France had asserted its views on Laos with the help of gunboats threatening Bangkok, was not easily forgotten. Britain had played a similar imperial game. When in

1909 the small states in the middle Malay peninsula were given up to British protection, much was lost for very little advantage. Yet, when in the early 1890s Siam's north-western border was defined at the impulse of the British Burma government, very little was lost. That remained true when in 1895 the northern frontier was sealed off at the point where newly-enlarged British Burma met newly-French Laos; there, with the sacrifice of two small tributary states, Britain and France were induced to let Siam remain independent.

Meanwhile, there was increasing cultural and educational contact with Britain. British tutors and advisers were a familiar sight at court; selected young Siamese, many of them from the vastly ramified royal family, attended British public schools and universities. The King's youngest full brother Prajadhipok, who had just left Eton for officer training at Woolwich when war broke out in 1914, begged King George V in vain to allow him to go on active service. Siamese contacts with France were more limited, but here, too, Siamese students could be found, nearly all of them scholarship students rather than scions of the nobility, enjoying both the intellectual and worldly pleasures of Paris.

King Vajiravudh personally favoured alliance with Britain, where he had studied, and he was anxious that Siam should play its part in the world as a modern nation state. Nationalism in his terms included readiness to fight for one's country and for the right side. If there were any doubt, Vajiravudh was not alone in being ready to make known his views on which side, in this European war, was the right side. One of his uncles, the venerable Buddhist patriarch and theologian Vajiranana, proclaimed in a well-argued address in 1916 that Buddhists must be prepared to fight in a just war. The speech was published in English translation and attracted the attention of Harcourt

Butler, Lieutenant-Governor of British Burma. Butler, prophet of the 'Imperial Idea', found Vajiranana's speech so apposite that he circulated copies to local administrators throughout Burma to be used as propaganda in favour of the war effort.

None of this was enough in itself to bring Siam into the distant conflict; by default, therefore, neutrality was the initial choice. It was only in 1917 that a decision imposed itself. On 6 April of that year the United States joined the war – one more country with which Siam had had long-standing relations and close economic ties. It may be no coincidence that a gift to *The Times* Red Cross Fund by 'the people of Siam' arrived two weeks later,[1] a timely reminder of where the King's personal sympathies lay. The US decision was rapidly followed by the involvement of several American allies. What began as a European conflict had clearly become a world war. Hesitation at an end, Siam finally declared war on Germany and Austria on 22 July. German and Austrian expatriates became enemy aliens and were interned forthwith (to save trouble, they were soon afterwards dispatched into British custody in India). A military mission led by the King's trusted brother, Chakrabongse, was dispatched to Europe in early 1918. Siamese troops reached Marseille in August, just in time to participate in the last weeks of the war against Germany. They included motor-ambulance transport and an aviation corps.

A peace conference, at which the victors would establish their conditions for the treaties to be placed before the defeated, had been foreseen long before the end of the war came in sight. In January 1919 the Peace Conference would actually commence, and, at the insistence of the French Prime Minister, Georges Clemenceau, it would take place in Paris. A year earlier, in January 1918, President Wilson had formulated an agenda in his Fourteen Points (see panel, p 50). Siam's reward for participating in the war on the side of the Allies was its invitation to the Conference, with an allocation of two seats at plenary sessions. As the war drew to its end, one of the questions that posed itself to King Vajiravudh and his foreign minister was: who should represent Siam in Paris? Their choice would fall, perhaps surprisingly, on three career diplomats, led by the King's cousin, Prince Charoon.

Vajiravudh, aged twenty-nine, had succeeded to the throne in 1910 after the long reign of his father Chulalongkorn. A student of Sandhurst and of Christ Church, Oxford (with no degree but a long essay on the Polish monarchy to his credit) and something of an aesthete, he had developed strong opinions on Siam, the way it should be governed and how it should reassert its place in the world. His opinions differed markedly from those of many contemporaries: hence the nationalistic Wild Tiger corps, somewhere between a scout troop and a private army, that that he founded immediately after his accession, and the officers' revolt that broke out within two years of his accession. Administrative change ought to have been easy: he was an absolute monarch. It was difficult because he was a member of a numerous family, that supplied almost the whole upper tier of government from its own ranks. In such a family there was continual jostling for succession; there were always a few malcontents available to lead palace revolutions. He was particularly well-supplied with uncles (King Mongkut had 39 sons) of whom the most powerful were Damrong Rajanubhab, Interior Minister since 1894, and Devawongse, who had been appointed Foreign Minister in 1881 and had held that fief for the whole of Vajiravudh's lifetime. Both these formidable figures were well known internationally.

Another son of Mongkut, one who by now had had enough of government and was therefore on much easier terms with the young king, was Nares. A generation ago Uncle Nares had been a moderniser, almost a rebel. A junior minister in the 1870s, he afterwards became Siamese ambassador in London and while there naturally became close to his youngest half-brother, Svasti, the first Thai ever to go to Oxford. Svasti completed his law studies at Balliol in 1886; Nares was recalled in the same year. Back in Bangkok, these two addressed to their half-brother Chulalongkorn on 8 January 1887 a petition asking that Siam become a constitutional monarchy. He replied, gently and patiently explaining why it would not happen.[2] The two tearaways had senior ministerial posts ahead of them (among Chulalongkorn's wives were no fewer than three of Svasti's full sisters, which surely did his career no harm).

Prince Charoon (1875–1928) was the eldest son of Prince Nares and grandson of King Mongkut. An Old Harrovian, he became a junior minister, then a career diplomat. Thai ambassador in Paris from 1913, he was the senior Siamese delegate at the Paris Peace Conference 1919, and a representative at the League of Nations from 1920, from which he was recalled in 1927, the year before he died.

Charoon's real name was Charunsakdi. In 1915, by royal decree, Thai noble families adopted surnames, a token of the westernisation of Siam; thenceforth he was Charunsakdi Kridakon. He was nicknamed Charoon by his tutor Morant, and remained 'Prince Charoon' in all Western documents, from his registration at Harrow to his signatures on the treaties and instruments later placed before him as ambassador.

At the moment of his recall from Britain, Nares had decided that his own three sons should have an English education but had not yet done anything about it. His wife Subhab therefore stayed on in London to look for a tutor whose job would be to prepare the three boys for entrance to a public school. Helped by FW Verney, the Siamese embassy's English secretary (and by Verney's aunt, Florence Nightingale), Subhab fixed on Robert Morant, a university contemporary of Svasti with no money but a first in theology from New College, Oxford. Morant joined Subhab and the two elder boys, 'Charoon' and Bavo-radej, aged 11 and 9, on the voyage to Bangkok. They arrived on 6 January 1887.

'The first impression I had of him [Morant] was one of awe,' Prince Charoon recalled, 'as to me he appeared so enormous. However, within a few days after the steamer had sailed, he had by his tact and kindness, as well as knowledge of boys' characters, put us at ease with him, and soon a friendship, which became lifelong, had begun.' Morant thought Subhab 'a fine character', found Bavoradej 'rather a handful' (he was afterwards Minister of War), but liked Charoon. The youngest brother, Sresthasiri, who was already in Siam, 'required much patience to make him learn anything'. Morant was allocated a house on the family's Bangkok property, on the banks of the great river Mae Nam, and the boys lived there too. 'After tea', wrote Charoon, 'he usually took a long walk, and sometimes he took us with him … it was indeed violent exercise for us, as in order to keep up with his long stride, we were obliged to trot most of the time.' They worked as hard as Morant could make them: there was a lot of ground to cover before the Harrow entrance exam. 'The boys are so awfully and unspeakably slow,' he wrote to a college friend, 'that … I could scream at their laziness and lassitude and lack of energy and utter absence of concentration … They would not have the slightest respect for a man who lost his temper,' he added.[3]

After two years with Charoon and his brothers, Morant was selected by Prince Devawongse for a higher post, that of tutor to King Chulalongkorn's intended heir, Prince Vajirun-his; but there had at least been time to prepare Charoon for the next stage in his career. He passed the Harrow exam and spent the next several years in England, destined at first for a career in the government. When the high-flying lawyer Prince

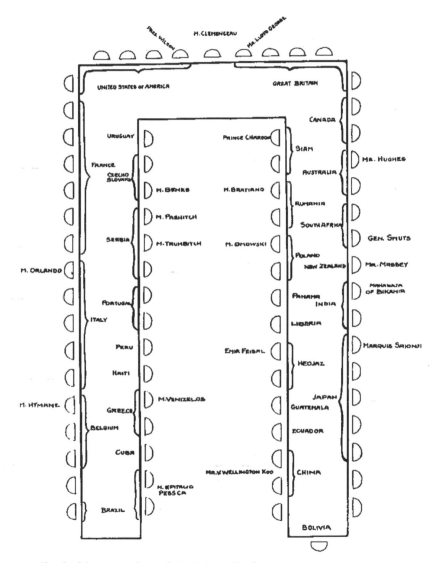

Sketch of the seating plan at the Paris Peace Conference.

Rabi attempted to make the Siamese Ministry of Justice something more than an arm of royal power – an instrument of objective justice, in effect – it was Charoon who was chosen as deputy minister by King Chulalongkorn with the special task of keeping an eye on Rabi. From this uncomfortable appointment it may have been a relief to escape into the diplomatic service. He served in Lisbon, Madrid and London, where one of his duties was to cajole Eton College into admitting young Prajadhipok. In 1906, still aged only thirty-one, Charoon was appointed *chargé d'affaires* in Paris; he was minister (ambassador) by 1913. By 1919, he was very comfortable there. Since Siam was at first neutral, even the First World War impinged rather little on the humdrum work of the Embassy. This might have changed during 1918 with the arrival of the Thai military mission, its motor-ambulances and its air corps, but these forces were led by the King's brother Chakrabongse and made few demands on Charoon. He still had plenty of time to keep up the embassy's paternal supervision of the Siamese students in France and had encouraged them to set up a society, Association Siamoise d'Intellectualité et d'Assistance Mutuelle (or, more memorably, *SIAM*).

Vajiravudh may have toyed with the idea of representing Siam personally in Paris. If so, it was only a passing thought. It was true that other heads of state were to be present – notably President Woodrow Wilson of the United States – but there would be no other hereditary monarchs. However modernistic his political aims, however Europhile and liberal his cultural attitudes, Vajiravudh would have been a fish out of water. And there was, after all, little of significance to be achieved. Germany and Austria had practically nothing that Siam wanted. This, surely, was the main consideration that led Vajiravudh and his foreign minister Devawongse to their decision. By comparison with the delegations of most other countries, Siam's would be noticeably modest: no head of state; no head of government; no cabinet minister, serving or even retired. Siam's delegation consisted of three diplomats led by its Old Harrovian ambassador in Paris, Prince Charoon, now aged 43. With him would be his 35-year-old cousin Prince Traidos, who had briefly served as ambassador to the United States before being appointed Deputy Foreign Minister to his father in 1913. The third delegate, 56 years old, belonged not to the royal Chakri dynasty but to a family of Portuguese merchants who had settled in Siam a hundred years earlier, in 1820:[4] Phya Bibadh Kosha had served as Siam's ambassador in Italy, but was fluent in English and he would be responsible at the Conference for negotiations with Britain.

Traidos Phrabandhu or **Devawongse II** (1883–1943) was the son of Prince Devawongse. A diplomat, he was booked to travel on the *Titanic* but missed the boat. He was deputy foreign minister from 1913, delegate to Paris Peace Conference in 1919. He succeeded his father as Foreign Minister in 1923, and recalled Charoon from Paris in 1927. He became privy councillor in 1931 and was dismissed in 1932 at the inception of constitutional monarchy.

Phya Bibadh Kosha (1863–1922), also known as Celestino Maria Xavier, was the grandson of Portuguese merchant Joachim Maria Xavier. He was educated in England. He had a junior post at the Siamese Embassy in Paris, then returned to Siam; 'Permanent Under-Secretary of State' in 1908. He was ambassador to Italy during First World War and a delegate to the Paris Peace Conference in 1919.

There was, however, one item on the wish list. Germany was among the countries that had an 'unequal treaty' with Siam. Negotiated during the 19th century, when Siam under Mongkut and Chulalongkorn was struggling to maintain national freedom, these treaties had bestowed 'extraterritorial' privileges on the subjects of certain powerful states. When the first such treaty was signed between Britain and Siam in 1855 its wide future implications were not foreseen (and Siamese justice had not begun to be reformed on European lines). By 1914, the unequal treaties conferred tax and duty exemptions, trial by consular courts for alleged offences in Siam, special trading rights and other immunities not only on visitors and businessmen from the eleven countries involved, but also on the people of their Asian colonies: thus, for example, large numbers of migrants from Indochina, Burma, Malaya and the Dutch Indies had valuable rights in Siam that natives lacked. These treaties diminished the country's independence and sometimes made it impossible to comply with new international obligations. The first signs of renegotiation are seen in the 1904 and 1907 treaties with France and the 1909 treaty with Britain, but in these Siam was still anything but an equal partner. In the latter, for example, Siam gave up all rights on the three most northerly Malay states, Kedah (including Perlis), Kelantan and Terengganu, all of which the British had recognised as Siamese in an earlier treaty of 1826. In return, Siam got little else but an assurance, of doubtful value, that Britain would not lay claim to more.

Vajiravudh had inherited a country with modernised laws and institutions; one of his long-term policy aims, in which Devawongse concurred, was to revise the treaties. It would be the Paris delegates' task to ensure that the unequal treaty with Germany was abrogated and to make all possible progress in renegotiating the other ten. This should now be easier, Devawongse felt, given Siam's newly strong moral position as a participant in the closing stages of the First World War.[5]

Negotiations with France had begun in Bangkok in early 1918, led by the French ambassador, Pierre Lefèvre-Pontalis. On the Siamese side Devawongse, as Foreign Minister, entrusted the detail to his son, Prince Traidos. If initial progress in the French negotiations was slow, this was not Traidos' fault.

Pontalis lacked the favour of the influential French Governor-General of Indochina, Albert Sarraut, who had him recalled.[6] The result of the upheaval was to shift the focus of the negotiations to Paris, where, on the Siamese side, Prince Traidos had been appointed to the second seat at the Peace Conference. On the French side, the permanent secretary of the foreign ministry, Philippe Berthelot, took personal charge, in close touch with Sarraut, who in May 1919 was back in Paris having completed his term as Governor-General.

Prince Charoon now took on the negotiations regarding Germany. Of the three Siamese representatives, he had the easiest task. As the defeated party the Germans did not take part in the Paris negotiations: as long as the abrogation of their extraterritorial rights in Siam was included in the draft treaty, all that was necessary would have been done. The draft contained many clauses that struck closer to Germany's heart than its trade and consular relations with distant Siam: over this issue no difficulties were raised. Under the Treaty of Versailles, signed by Charoon on Siam's behalf in the Hall of Mirrors on 28 June, Siam's 'unequal' treaty obligations to Germany were formally stated to have terminated on the date of Siam's declaration of war, 22 July 1917. 'To have this in black and white, signed by all the allied nations as well as the enemy',[7] was a big step for Siam, Charoon justifiably claimed.

One of the principal tasks of the Conference was to prepare the ground for the League of Nations. Siam was to be among the founding members. President Wilson laboured hard for the League, and though he failed to get his own country to sign up to it, Siam's presence and ready participation undoubtedly helped to ease its treaty renegotiation with the United States. Recording a meeting with the three delegates, Wilson wrote to Frank L Polk, acting Secretary of State, that 'on this subject of

CLAUSES RELATING TO SIAM IN THE TREATY OF VERSAILLES

135. Germany recognises that all treaties, conventions and agreements between her and Siam, and all rights, title and privileges derived therefrom, including all rights of extraterritorial jurisdiction, terminated as from 22 July 1917.

136. All goods and property in Siam belonging to the German Empire or to any German State, with the exception of premises used as diplomatic or consular residences or offices, pass *ipso facto* and without compensation to the Siamese Government. The goods, property and private rights of German nationals in Siam shall be dealt with in accordance with the provisions of Part X (Economic Clauses) of the present Treaty.

137. Germany waives all claims against the Siamese Government on behalf of herself or her nationals arising out of the seizure or condemnation of German ships, the liquidation of German property, or the internment of German nationals in Siam. This provision shall not affect the rights of the parties interested in the proceeds of any such liquidation, which shall be governed by the provisions of Part X (Economic Clauses) of the present Treaty.

surrender of extraterritoriality [I] feel that there is a great deal of force in their contentions'; he wanted to go 'as far as it is prudent and possible at the present moment' in meeting their wishes. Accordingly a new treaty between the United States and Siam, replacing the 'unequal' treaty of 1856, was finally signed on 18 December 1920. Under this, US citizens and businesses in Siam ceased to claim the special legal and economic privileges granted during the 19th century.[8]

The third delegate, Phya Bibadh Kosha, urged similar concessions on Britain; so did the King himself, who discussed the matter with the British ambassador in Bangkok. Traidos focused on the French. But progress in both cases was elusive. Britain and France had impoverished themselves in the First World War. They needed to re-establish their national finances. German reparations would be the major element in this, but more was needed. The *mise en valeur* of the French colonies, urged by Albert Sarraut, may be seen as characterising a means to this end: economic development from which not only the colonies would benefit, but principally the mother country. Siam was not a British or French colony but was seen in a similar light, as virgin territory for development. French businesses based in Indochina wanted economic openings in Siam, as many as possible and on the best possible terms; British businesses, from bases in India, Singapore and the Far East, wanted exactly the same. Neither was prepared to say this openly; instead, both identified difficulties over the Siamese legal system and refused to give up extraterritoriality – and thus to complete the negotiations – until these difficulties were solved. Japan, by contrast, anxious to gain influence in South East Asia, meanwhile agreed readily enough in 1923. The United States having been the first to give up the old horse-trading, largely at Woodrow Wilson's impulse,[9] perhaps it needed a Wilsonian voice to shame the European diplomats into compliance. The successful conclusion of the long negotiations with France and Britain, and of similar agreements with the other countries, is credited largely to Francis B Sayre, an international lawyer and Wilson's son-in-law, appointed as Siam's Adviser in Foreign Affairs in late 1923. Two years of dogged negotiation by Sayre in European capitals reached a climax in Rome in August 1925. Italy had been the most reluctant of all, but after a last interview with Mussolini, Sayre was able to assure King Vajiravudh by telegram that 'all treaty powers are now agreed to surrender old territorial rights. Siam's complete autonomy is now regained. I rejoice that she has now again come into her own.'[10]

At the end of the Paris Peace Conference, Traidos returned to Siam, where he was to become foreign minister on his father's death in 1923. Phya Bibadh Kosha, ambassador to Italy, had only two years left to live. Charoon remained in Europe. Still ambassador to France, he henceforth doubled as Siam's first delegate to the League of Nations in Geneva, where he was a regular presence from the first General Assembly in November 1920. For Siam, as for many other members, the real benefit of the League was that it centralised and facilitated

'Siam's complete autonomy is now regained. I rejoice that she has now again come into her own.'

FRANCIS B SAYRE TO KING VAJIRAVUDH, AUGUST 1925

the discussion of an ever-increasing number of international agreements on commercial and administrative issues. Among others, Charoon's signature is found on the International Convention for the Suppression of the Traffic in Women and Children, Geneva, 30 September 1921; on the International Opium Convention, Geneva, 19 February 1925; and the International Convention for the Abolition of Import and Export Prohibitions and Restrictions, signed in November 1927 and possibly his last.

In 1921 the Siamese legation in Paris acquired a new assistant secretary, Wichit Wathakan, a self-taught writer and linguist, child of a part-Chinese trading family near Uthai Thani. Part of his task was to accompany Charoon to League of Nations assemblies, presence at which (he afterwards said) was like attending the best university in the world.[11] Wichit also found himself dealing, day to day, with the Siamese students in Paris, most of whom benefited from allowances paid by the government and whose activities it was the embassy's task to monitor.

King Vajiravudh died in November 1925 three months after receiving Sayre's triumphant telegram. He had no son (and until two days before his death no daughter either; his difficulties with women were the subject of scandal). His three next younger full brothers had all predeceased him (the trusted

Chakrabongse succumbed to Spanish flu on a visit to Singapore in June 1920). Passing over their children, Vajiravudh sensibly named his one surviving brother, Prajadhipok, as his successor.

Thus it was Prajadhipok who during the Siamese New Year celebrations 18 months later welcomed the newly-signed treaties with Sweden, Italy, Norway, Belgium and Luxembourg that marked the end of Francis Sayre's labours, the end of the inequality, and the complete recovery of Siam's judicial and administrative autonomy.[12] At a state banquet Prajadhipok spoke – a diminutive and disarmingly modest figure – to an audience of princes and officials. Siam, he said, had attained a new standing among the nations. The first three kings of the Chakri dynasty had fought against the enemies on their frontiers as in olden days: the danger that had to be guarded against came from possible foreign invaders. Then came a new danger, springing from the country's more intimate connection with European nations. That danger Siam's neighbours were unable to resist; they succumbed and became dependencies of European powers. Siam alone was able to save her independence, thanks to the sagacity and ability of the second three kings of the dynasty.

> 'Siam's neighbours were unable to resist the danger; they succumbed and became dependencies of European powers. Siam alone was able to save her independence.'
> KING PRAJADHIPOK, 1927

It was to be regretted, he added, that King Vajiravudh, who had brought this development almost to its end, had not lived to see the completion of his labours. On an altar beside him stood golden caskets containing the relics of the three preceding kings – Mongkut, Chulalongkorn and Vajiravudh – placed there, said Prajadhipok, so that all those present might make, as it were, an offering to these august predecessors of the knowledge of what their labours had now accomplished.[13] The legacy of Vajiravudh is highly controversial, but Prajadhipok was right to give him credit. In this renegotiation of the treaties Vajiravudh did a great deal for the survival and future prosperity of Siam. Just one detail, that of the right to set import duties, was left for future statesmen to settle.

Siam remained an absolute monarchy. The origins of the constitutional change that eventually came during Prajadhipok's brief reign can be traced to Paris in the early 1920s, to the very group of Siamese students whose activities were supervised by Charoon and his assistant, Wichit Wathakan. One of these students, from 1920 onwards, was Pridi Phanomyong, a 'scholarship boy' with a family background not unlike Wichit Wathakan's, born near the old ruined capital of Ayutthaya. He was to study politics and eventually to gain a doctorate in law at the Sorbonne. Pridi himself traced his early political enthusiasms to the overthrow of the Manchu dynasty in China in 1911 and the emergence of Sun Yatsen; then to the Russian Revolution; then again to communist stirrings among Asian and colonial students in Paris, the same movement in which Hồ Chí Minh was prominent. A second student was Plaek Kittasangka

Pridi Phanomyong (1900–1983) studied in Caen and Paris 1921–7. He organised the 1932 coup. He was foreign minister; regent for King Ananda Mahidol; became Prime Minister in 1946, but highly unpopular after the King's unexplained death. He was ousted in 1947 and retreated to exile in China and (after 1970) France.

Prayun Pamonmontri (1897–1982) studied in Paris 1922–7; participated in the 1932 and 1933 coups. He was a consul in Saigon. He became a member of Thai-Japanese Military Commission and was imprisoned as a collaborator 1945–6.

Plaek Kittasangka or **Pibul Songgram** (1897–1964), undertook artillery studies at Fontainebleau; participated in the 1932 coup. He was prime minister from 1938–45 (latterly in alliance with Japan) and from 1948–57. He was ousted by a coup and retreated to exile in Japan where he died.

(later known as Pibul), son of a durian grower on the edge of Bangkok, now attending the artillery school at Fontainebleau. A third was Prayun Pamonmontri, half-Siamese, half-German, who had been one of Vajiravudh's pages and then drifted through Europe before settling to study politics in Paris.

Prayun was the first to cross Charoon's path: perhaps fearing the revolutionary fervour of their organisation, the ambassador forbade a student group to go to London for a joint meeting with the association of Siamese students in England. That association had been sedulously encouraged by the future King Vajiravudh, a member and contributor to its magazine during his student days; it was still flourishing, and Prayun (whose allowance did not come via the embassy, perhaps rather from Vajiravudh himself) flouted the ban and went to London anyway.

Then, in 1926, the Paris students, led by Pridi and backed by Wichit Wathakan, petitioned via Charoon for an increase in their allowance. Charoon's reaction, in correspondence with King Prajadhipok, was sharp. When he had founded *SIAM*, he wrote, he 'did not intend it to become a political club' and had forbidden embassy officials to join it. Wichit had disobeyed this order. He was taking a very active part in the student group and he and Pridi 'were running it as they liked. I consider Vichitr [Wichit] a dangerous man and ought to be kept under observation. He is very ambitious.'[14] As for Pridi, he had been talking to his fellow-students about revolution and was a 'danger to the throne'.[15] Charoon recommended the student's immediate recall to Bangkok.

King Prajadhipok at first agreed with Charoon. But by time-honoured tradition Siamese subjects, however humble their status, were entitled to petition the monarch. On this occasion, after hearing a personal appeal by Pridi's father, Prajadhipok countermanded his earlier order. Pridi should be allowed to complete his doctorate; he was 'intelligent but inclined to be a little brash,' the King noted privately. 'Once he enters the government in a responsible position he will probably work well, and I don't much believe that he will become a "serious danger to the throne" as Prince Charunsakdi has reported.' [16] Prajadhipok and his Foreign Minister, Prince Traidos, then had to decide what to do about Wichit Wathakan, whose relationship with his ambassador had clearly broken down. The decision was to move Wichit to London and to promote him to Secretary.

The thinking behind these decisions is not known, but the world of Thai diplomats and expatriates was a small one. It is surely relevant that Devawongse personally liked Wichit, and that Devawongse's son Traidos had worked alongside Charoon in 1919. It is surely relevant that in the early 1920s Prajadhipok himself, not yet considered a likely heir to the throne, spent a short time pursuing his military training at the Ecole Supérieure de la Guerre in Paris: he had therefore experienced Charoon's supervision of the Siamese students in Paris at first hand. As if to complete the demonstration that Charoon had used up his credit, less than a year later he was accused of misappropriating a proportion of the funds intended for the Siamese students' allowances and was recalled to Bangkok. He withdrew to the fine new house in Bangkok that King Vajiravudh had commissioned and presented to his father Nares in 1917. Nares had died in 1925, and Charoon died soon after he returned to Siam in October 1928.

Charoon was right, of course. There really had been seditious talk among the Siamese students in Paris, and his loss of authority when the King changed his mind made it all the easier for Pridi, Pibul and Prayun to gather a more formal group of like-minded students, who began in February 1927 to meet at Prayun's lodgings in the rue de Sommerard on the Left Bank. They were 'promoters' of revolution; Pibul was 'captain', Pridi the real animator, Prayun the secretary. An honorary member was Phra Sarasat, a critic of the Siamese government who was in France as a refugee. The students had been specifically forbidden to meet him; perhaps they obeyed, but they kept in touch with him in writing.

Assuming (as they all did) that Siam must change, the question before them was how to effect this change. A popular revolution would not happen. There were no revolutionary masses to bring it about. The need, then, would be to institute change from above: a seizure of power, a *coup d'état*. With their sights fixed on this interesting prospect the students of 1927 returned from Paris to Bangkok, where the scholarship system guaranteed prestigious placings for them. Pridi took a post in the Ministry of Justice with an attached lecturership at Chulalongkorn University. Pibul was to teach at the military academy and serve as aide-de-camp to a member of the Supreme Council. Another member of the group was to lecture at the naval academy. A contemporary, Khuang Abhaiwongse, joined the post and telegraph service.[17] Abhaiwongse had not attended the Paris meetings – he was studying in Lyon – but proved to be a sympathiser in spite of his very different background. He was the son of the last hereditary governor of Battambang (ceded to French-ruled Cambodia in 1907) and the uncle of Suvadhana, least unlucky of the wives of King Vajiravudh.

In the first years of Prajadhipok's reign there was no change at all. The King's ministers all agreed that Siam was not yet ready for representative government; even Traidos, who in 1931 was asked by the King to help to draw up a possible constitution, did not believe in his task; even Prince Purachatra, the King's charismatic half-brother and Siam's great moderniser, took the same view. In 1929 Purachatra was in Berlin and London to inaugurate Siam's wireless communication with Europe, and talked with Sir Samuel Hoare (they had been at Harrow together) about linking Siam with the British Imperial air mail service.[18] Purachatra, a railway enthusiast, rather discouraged roadbuilding, but there was talk of a new road bridge across the wide Mae Nam river. In August King Prajadhipok visited Singapore and Jakarta and found, slightly to his hosts' surprise, that as the only independent monarch in South East Asia he was unexpectedly popular with the crowds.

It was the world financial crisis that sparked change. Discontent began to simmer at the dangerous effect on Siam's economy and thence on the lives of those least able to weather any such crisis, notably the many rice farmers whose income depended on exports to the British Empire. Britain had abandoned the Gold Standard; Siam attempted to maintain it, with disastrous consequences. Since lack of money appeared to be the problem, popular attention began to focus on the vast royal family, its apparent indolence and perceived vast wealth.

There were ominous predictions that the Chakri dynasty would end in its 150th year. And yet the celebrations of the 150th anniversary, on 6 April 1932, passed smoothly. The Rama I road bridge, named after the royal ancestor, was ceremonially opened; it linked Bangkok, Rama I's new capital, across the Mae Nam with the monastery city of Thonburi where the short-lived preceding dynasty had held sway. But on 24 June, while the King was away at his summer resort of Hua Hin, those princes who happened to remain in Bangkok were rounded up at the Dusit Palace and held hostage by army officers. The resourceful Prince Purachatra alone evaded capture: he hijacked a railway engine and sped off to Hua Hin.

In this way the plans laid in Paris seven years earlier came to maturity. The prime movers were Pridi Phanomyong, who had been discussing things with the young lawyers of Bangkok, had drafted a constitution and was to take charge of propaganda; Khuang Abhaiwongse, who was excellently located in the postal service to ensure that communications were open when needed and cut when not; and Pibul. He, in spite of his sensitive position as princely equerry, had turned a band of well-placed army officers (27 of them, by one count) in or near Bangkok, along with a few navy men, into 'promoters' of the revolution.

The modest purpose, as announced to officer cadets and other troops gathered around the Dusit Palace, was to ask the King for a constitution. The ultimatum had already been sent. It urged the monarch 'to reign again as King under the constitutional monarchy established by the People's Party. If your Majesty refuses to accept the offer ... the People's Party will ... appoint another prince whom they consider to be efficient as King.' The threat was perhaps empty; in any case it was unnecessary. The King received conflicting advice from his ministers and afterwards claimed to have taken that of his wife and his mother-in-law. 'I am willing to co-operate,' he replied in essence, giving as reason his wish during his few remaining years to further the progress of the Thai people and to ensure that any new government would receive international recognition.[19]

The proposed constitution was socialist, even communist, in some of its provisions. It called for a People's Assembly (parliament) and People's Committee (cabinet) led by a Chairman (prime minister). Initially the parliament and cabinet were self-appointed; even after the planned elections, a large proportion of appointees was to remain. The King – educated in Europe as were those who plotted against him – immediately negotiated some sensible changes to the constitution, and after solemnly proclaiming it on 10 December 1932 remarked privately that (although he would not have chosen these particular ministers) he himself 'had thought out the details of such a ceremony for years, knowing that it will have to come in my lifetime … even the proclamation … had been drafted in my mind for a long time.'[20]

> 'I had thought out the details of such a ceremony for years, knowing that it would have to come in my lifetime.'
>
> KING PRAJADHIPOK AFTER FORMALLY PROCLAIMING SIAM'S CONSTITUTIONAL MONARCHY, 1932

Pridi's constitution additionally called for the government to buy all agricultural land; farmers were to become government employees. The King opposed this truly radical measure and the cabinet split on it. Guns were brandished in the Assembly. There followed a second coup in June 1933 after which, though the nationalisation of land was abandoned, Pridi emerged as Interior Minister. A royalist counter-coup four months later (not supported by the King) failed. The senior royal involved was Charoon's younger brother Bavoradej, who fled to French Indochina and spent many years in exile there. These traumatic events, with their aftermath in restrictive legislation and special courts, were more than enough for the King, who now left the country for an eye operation. He settled at Cranleigh in Surrey; on 2 March 1935, without returning to Siam, he abdicated, designating no successor.

The constitutional successor was his nephew, the ten-year-old Ananda Mahidol. The boy was then living at Lausanne with his mother and younger brother Bhumibol. He accepted the monarchy but remained at school in Switzerland; he was represented in Siam by a council of regents. It was not until late 1938 that he first visited his kingdom, and then only for a few months. His presence was ceremonially important, but politically it made little if any difference. By that time Pridi as Foreign Minister had successfully completed a further renegotiation of the foreign treaties, ending the last vestige of inequality in Siam's relation with foreign powers by securing the freedom to set the level of import duties. Pibul, after several years as power-broker behind the scenes, and after two assassination attempts, had finally taken the post of Prime Minister. Stability was in view. National pride was about to be massaged with the adoption of a new official name, a decision urged long before in the writings of Wichit Wathakan: *Prades Sayam*, 'land of Siam', has from 1939 been known as *Prades Thai* 'land of the Thai' (the slightly Germanic form *Thailand* was made official in English and other foreign languages). The young men who caused such headaches to Charoon had fulfilled their fondest dreams.

Manuel Luis Quezon the first President of the Philippines, escorts Clare Booth Luce to a reception at the Manila Hotel for her husband the publishing tycoon Henry Booth Luce in 1935.

III

The Legacy

From Resistance to Independence in South East Asia

The Paris Peace Conference in itself would have little direct consequence for the territories of South East Asia. Of all the issues in dispute in the region, Siam's renegotiation of its unequal treaties is the only one that had an impact on the Treaty of Versailles. The Conference's legacy in matters of self-determination, the rise of nationalism and the approach to independence would be more long-lasting, however.

The only direct and immediate response in South East Asia to the Paris Peace Conference occurred in Singapore, a British colony since the 1820s, where the Chinese community rose up in protest at the frustration of China's diplomatic aims. On 4 May 1919, students and workers in Beijing marched through the streets demanding the rejection of the Peace Conference's decisions, about to be enshrined in the Treaty of Versailles. The sticking point was the refusal to return Japanese-held Shandong to China; this would, indeed, impel the Chinese delegates in Paris, alone among the Allies, to refuse to sign the Treaty. On the days following the Paris decision, demonstrations and strikes took place in many parts of China, and the news spread

immediately to Singapore, whose influential Chinese community – one of the largest outside China – was galvanised into
action. There were widespread calls for an embargo of Japanese
businesses and products, backed
up by threats of violence. Rioting
erupted on 19 June; Japanese-
owned property was ransacked
and burned; two rioters and two
policemen (but no Japanese) were
killed. There were 130 arrests.
Smaller demonstrations continued for some days.

'We know that at the Paris
Peace Conference our
foreign delegates
announced their failures.
We overseas Chinese
deeply fear that from this
point it will not be long
until our nation is
destroyed.'

ANONYMOUS MANIFESTO
REPRINTED IN SINGAPORE FREE
PRESS (6 JUNE 1919)[1]

Nationalism was absent from
Singapore, indeed irrelevant to
it, as a city where the majority of
the population was not of local
origin. There were inter-ethnic tensions, but the British, colonialists though they might be, were not normally affected. Even
now, although the British had encouraged Japan's Twenty-One
Demands on China in 1915, and the British delegation in Paris
had been part of the pro-Japanese consensus, the British in Singapore were not targeted. They were, however, a small and vul-
nerable group, quick to defend their privileges and their dignity.
Thus Singapore's English-language press was incensed by disruption caused by 'Chinese hooligans', urged severe repression
and showed no inclination to understand the reasons behind
the protests.

The Governor, Sir Arthur Young, had been in post since 1912
and had thus observed the growth of Sun Yatsen's Guomindang
movement among the Chinese communities of Singapore and
Malaya, and its influence on the exiled Vietnamese communities of Indochina; but Sun aimed to revolutionise China and the

Guomindang had no local political programme. Sun himself had visited Singapore eight times between 1901 and 1911 and had treated the city as a base during his years of exile. British regulation until 1919 focused on discouraging open attacks on the Chinese government – Sun himself had once been expelled from Singapore for breaking this rule.[2]

The rioting of June 1919 having been quelled, Young quickly restored the position of Secretary for Chinese Affairs, normally held by a Briton with Chinese expertise, which had been cut from his establishment. Soon afterwards he left, his term as Governor over, to be replaced by Sir Laurence Guillemard. Guillemard and his expert advisers, none of them especially familiar with Singapore, were faced with the accurate intelligence that the Guomindang in China was now forging an alliance with the feared new international movement of Communism – not only with the infant Chinese communist party but, more ominously, with the Russians and the Comintern. The link (very tenuous in reality) between the Second Comintern Congress's anti-colonialism and the Singapore branch of the Guomindang became a guiding principle of local British thinking. In 1925, after wrangles with William Maxwell, Chief Secretary of the Federated Malay States, and long discussion with the Colonial Office, Guillemard succeeded in getting agreement that the Guomindang in Singapore and Malaya should be banned. From this point onwards, joining the newly underground organisation became an anti-British act.[3] In this strange way a colonial territory that offered no basis for nationalism, and was practically free of it, set the regional pattern of increasingly political polarisation that marked the last decades of colonial South East Asia.

The stories of Burma, the Philippines, French Indochina and the Dutch Indies, from the points at which we left them, run parallel through the 1920s and 1930s. The United States, unlike the other three colonial powers – France, the Netherlands and Britain – had accepted in principle that independence would come to the Philippines, yet all four of them had dreams of 'association', which in practice meant that they aimed to grant a measure of autonomy while retaining political suzerainty and commercial influence. In all four territories a local political elite, apparently prepared to favour 'association', had been fostered by means of elective assemblies.

In all four, attempts were made to eliminate, exclude or sideline the radicals. It never quite worked. Success came closest in the case of the Philippines, where, uniquely, friendly association between the colonial power and the colonised was destined to continue to the present day. Even there, however, radical heroes were not quite forgotten. The Philippine Independence Missions to the United States in the 1920s and early 1930s would often call at Yokohama in Japan on their way to and from the United States and would make a point of visiting the Karihan Cafe at 149 Yamashita-cha, run by Artemio Ricarte, the Philippine insurrectionist who, having escaped arrest by the British and Americans in 1915, had made his way to Japan, where he would live in exile for the next twenty-six years. Meagre profits from the restaurant were supplemented by occasional gifts from Manuel Quezon.[4]

In Vietnam the Việt Quốc or VNQDD, beginning in 1927, built up a clandestine organisation within the country, emulating the Guomindang. Suffering under fierce repression, the Việt Quốc boldly arranged a mutiny of Vietnamese troops at Yên Bái, north of Hanoi, on 10 February 1930. Momentarily it looked dangerous; it was rapidly suppressed, but French nervousness is demonstrated not only by the 80 death sentences that followed, but also by the fact that immediately afterwards up to

10,000 troops, 80 per cent of the total strength, were moved to new locations. The 1930s in Indochina were peaceful on the surface, resistance within the country having apparently been cowed. Phan Bội Châu, after many years of retirement under mild house arrest, died in 1940. The journalist Nguyễn An Ninh, the most prominent of those who tried to bring change to French Indochina without violence, was to die of beriberi on Côn Sơn prison island in 1943.

The French administration in Indochina, weakened in June 1940 when France signed its armistice with Germany, was compelled in September to accept Japanese occupation, almost completing the encirclement of China and preparing the ground for advances on Malaya and Burma.

Under Pibul's leadership the newly-named Thailand, sensing this weakness, invaded Cambodia and Laos in October 1940, whose seizure by France in 1893 had never been forgotten. The invasion faltered and it was Japan that gained, imposing a settlement and in the course of 1941 gradually reducing Thailand to submission. Japan occupied Thailand in December 1941.

Burma, meanwhile, after the London discussions of 1919 and 1920 in the shadow of the Paris Peace Conference, had emerged as a governor's province in Britain's Indian Empire. For the next fifteen years the country was ruled under a form of dyarchy that still allowed British administrators the upper hand. During the first decade Burma remained relatively quiet, very much as if the negotiations had brought results capable of satisfying both sides; and yet the extremely low turnout at successive elections was evidence that most Burmese saw no benefit in the seesaw of party majorities and disputatious cabinets. During this period May Oung served as Home Minister for two years before his sudden death in 1926 at the age of 46. Surface tranquillity ended in the widespread Saya San rebellion of 1930, led, as had been the case on some earlier occasions, by a charismatic Buddhist monk. Saya San was executed in 1931; the uprising was ruthlessly suppressed. The popular support it had gathered served as a reminder that under the surface Burma was as restless as ever. The atmosphere is uncomfortably evoked in George Orwell's *Burmese Days* (1934; fictional, but so close to reality that publication was delayed in Britain for fear of libel action) and in Maurice Collis's memoir *Trials in Burma* (1938): as District Magistrate of Rangoon in 1929–30 Collis had found himself defending a colonial government in which he could no longer believe.

At the very moment of Saya San's execution, in November 1931, the so-called Burma Round Table Conference took place in London, an attempt to determine future colonial policy in parallel with the much-boycotted India Round Table Conferences of 1930–2. Among Burmese delegates was one woman, May Oung's daughter, Mya Sein, predictably nicknamed 'Miss May Oung' in the British press. The 1931 discussions led with agonising slowless to a constitutional milestone of 1937. In that year, separated finally from India, Burma became a Crown Colony with a new constitution calling for a fully elected assembly.

Chit Hlaing, whose power and popularity had declined in the mid-1920s, was in London for King George VI's coronation in 1937; he lived until 1952. Ba Pe, having served as Education Minister and Home Minister, was gaoled in 1941, shortly before the Japanese occupation, and disappears from the record. By the late 1930s other Burmese politicians were taking the political lead, such as Ba Maw and U Saw, two lawyers celebrated for their unsuccessful defence of Saya San. Ba Maw held office from 1937 to 1939 as Burma's first prime minister; U Saw served in the same role from 1940 until the eve of the Japanese invasion. Rangoon fell to the Japanese on 7 March 1942.

Henk Sneevliet had returned from China in 1923 to the Dutch communist movement in which he had served his apprenticeship. Both he and Baars were to fall victim to the German occupation: Sneevliet joined the resistance and was executed at Amersfoort in 1942, while Baars died at Auschwitz in 1944. Meanwhile, in the Dutch Indies the general collapse of communist organisation and the exile of every one of the leaders of the early 1920s left the way clear for Sukarto's non-communist Indonesian National Party, founded in 1927. This in turn met determined repression, and very little progress towards self-government was made during the 1930s; but the Netherlands, under German occupation from May 1940, could do nothing to defend the Indies against Japan. Opposition to the Japanese advance by American, British and allied troops was swept away during January and February 1942.

To complete the regional picture, Japanese forces attacked Malaya and Hong Kong in December 1941. Singapore fell on 15 February 1942. The attack on the Philippines (distantly foreseen in Warren Harding's questioning of Manuel Quezon in Washington in 1919) had begun on 8 December 1941; the US surrender followed five months later. Thus, all four colonial territories were engulfed, while Thailand became a Japanese satellite. Local politicians had choices to make. Some actively encouraged the Japanese advance, foreseeing that this upheaval would bring independence nearer. Most eventually worked with them, gaining what national advantage they could. The long-term exiles who were already in Japan fared variously; Cường Đế, for decades a figurehead-in-waiting for a government of Indochina, never achieved that position. Artemio Ricarte came home, and in fact died in the Philippines as the Japanese were being driven out, in a last heroic attempt to fight the returning Americans. Of the exiles whose politics put them in opposition to Japan, Musso, the only still-faithful exiled communist of the Dutch Indies, stayed away from the region during the war; but in February 1941, in the confusion of the Japanese advance, Hồ Chí Minh (a name he had now adopted) at last crossed the border from southern China and established a bridgehead on Indochina's northern frontier.

Throughout the region the Japanese invasion was the event that brought change. Thailand's tortuous path is symbolised by the fate of the house built for Prince Nares in 1917, Charoon's home during the last two years of his life. After his brother Bavoradej fled into exile in 1933, it was assigned as lodging for a series of royal and state guests. In 1942 it was allocated to Prayun Pamonmontri, who as army commander worked closely with the Japanese during that period. In 1944 it passed to Charoon's former student adversary Pridi Phanomyong; thus in this house the 'Free Thai' opposition to the Japanese was co-ordinated and the country was prepared for its swift change of course towards American alliance after the Japanese defeat. Thailand suffers regular *coups d'état*; it was as a result of two such incidents, in 1947 and 1957, that Pridi and Pibul in turn fled the country and died in exile. As yet the Chakri dynasty is unshaken. As a haven of relative stability the country has become a hub of international organisations, and Prince Nares' house is now the Food and Agriculture Organization regional library for Asia and the Pacific.[5]

The Dutch attempted to regain the Indies after the Japanese defeat, but the struggle was beyond them. Tan Malaka, who had continued to serve the Comintern from abroad, did not return to Indonesia until 1942; Darsono in 1950; Semaun, who remained in the Netherlands as PKI's representative to the Dutch communist party, not until 1956. Musso eventually returned from Japan to lead an abortive uprising in 1948 in which he met his death. The position of the more moderate Sukarno was by that time unassailable. Indonesia became independent in 1949.

The French fought their way back into Indochina in 1945 but found Hồ Chí Minh in a strong bargaining position, particularly in the northern half of Vietnam. Nguyễn Hải Thần's nationalists were part of his united front, and Thần was fleetingly vice-president in 1946 (thus, after all vicissitudes, an alliance such as Lenin proposed in 1920 was the winning strategy). The French held on doggedly for nine years, building on the division between north and south and drawing the United States into the struggle. In the south they set up the former Emperor Bảo Đại as president. Reluctantly they relinquished their two protectorates, Cambodia and Laos, in 1953 and 1954; in the same year the disastrous defeat of Điện Biên Phủ led directly to their withdrawal from Vietnam, leaving the Americans to fight on unavailingly for nineteen years more. The country was united, six years after Hồ's death, in 1975.

> 'Our revolution has lasted three years and there is still nothing that the peasants, workers, youth, and women have gained from it.'
>
> MUSSO, RADIO BROADCAST, SEPTEMBER 1948[6]

As an early sign that the changeover would be friendly in the Philippines, Francis Harrison, now married to his fifth wife after two more divorces, returned to the country on 12 October 1934. He was greeted at the harbour by Manuel Quezon, Rafael Palma, Jaime de Veyra and other former members of his cabinets, and spent much of the following eight years as political adviser to Quezon, who by this time was President of the 'Commonwealth of the Philippines' under United States suzerainty. Quezon's last, ignoble fight, in exile in Washington during the Japanese occupation, was the attempt to retain his presidency beyond the appointed term; had he given it up, an election being impossible, he would have been replaced by his vice-president Osmeña. He won the fight but was already dying of tuberculosis. On his death in 1944, at a health resort in New York state, he was succeeded by Osmeña in any case.[7] Only in the Philippines did an exiled administration return after the Japanese defeat to take control definitively, and the Philippines achieved full independence in 1946. Osmeña himself then joined the category of wartime leaders who fail to be re-elected when the war is over.

In Burma Ba Maw had served a second term as Prime Minister under Japanese domination, fled to Japan, and, when Japan fell, spent a year in American captivity. U Saw travelled to London in November 1941 to urge Dominion status for Burma, was found to have kept in touch with the Japanese as well, and spent the next four years interned in Uganda. The British returned triumphant to Burma but gave in rather quickly, and independence in 1948 marked a very sharp break, further evidence if any were needed of the clash of cultures that had seen the British and Burmese ever at odds. The footwear issue had hit where it hurt. This was already evident from early British responses in which health concerns ('Europeans who respect themselves or their health do not visit the pagoda platform'[8]) and cultural slurs (the 'beastly bare feet' of an Indian in a 1920s novel[9]) attempted to screen the loss of face. It was never forgotten. On entering Buddhist precincts in Burma one still sees the unobtrusive but uncompromising words 'NO FOOTWEARING' – a reminder of the historic dispute of 1917 in which a Burmese political movement first learned that it could oppose the colonialists and win.

The roots of anti-colonialism in early 20th-century South East Asia were religious, economic, social and political; local *causes célèbres* such as footwear in Burma and long hair in Vietnam served to crystallise opinion. But events in the world beyond South East Asia during these years played a crucial role in spreading the ideas of resistance and of future independence. Japan's victory in its war with Russia, in 1905, a victory of Asians over Europeans, was an immediate inspiration in Burma and throughout the region. The Russian Revolution in 1917, the founding of the Communist International, and the new emphasis on revolution in colonial territories, galvanised Indonesians, Vietnamese and others. President Wilson's Fourteen Points, in January 1918, spoke more clearly to colonial peoples across the world than Wilson intended. The Peace Conference of 1919, for which the Fourteen Points provided a kind of agenda, directly aided Siam's quest to regain complete sovereignty. The Peace Conference was also the recipient of Vietnamese independence claims, and in the same year, for the first time, delegations dispatched from the Philippines and Burma to their respective 'imperial' capitals demanded progress towards independence. Independence was slow to come, but the developments of these years made its coming inevitable.

Notes

Prologue: The Indochina Delegate

1. Hồ Chí Minh, *Ecrits 1920–1969* (Éditions en Langues Etrangères, Hanoi: 1971) pp 11–13; Jean Charles *et al* (eds), *Le congrès de Tours* (Éditions Sociales, Paris: 1980) pp 326–7. Fuller quotation in Thu Trang-Gaspard, *Hồ Chí Minh à Paris* (L'Harmattan, Paris: 1992) pp 121–2.

2. Sophie Quinn-Judge in *Ho Chi Minh: the missing years* (Hurst, London: 2003) p 16, credits Pierre Guesde with this work; Patrice Morlat in *Les affaires politiques de l'Indochine 1895–1923: les grandes commis: du savoir au pouvoir* (L'Harmattan, Paris: 1995) pp 294–301 ascribes it to Guesde's expert assistant Przyluski, whose early career he traces fully.

3. In standard Vietnamese orthography. In his earliest known signatures the spelling is Nguyen Ai Quac (see panel, p. x).

4. *Revendications du peuple annamite*; compare the translation in Marvin E Gentlemen and others, *Vietnam and America: a documented history* (Grove Press, New York: 1985). William Duiker in *Ho Chi Minh* (Hyperion,

New York: 2000) offers a narrative of Hồ Chí Minh
pacing the corridors of the Palace of Versailles to deliver
this petition. It didn't happen; the Conference took place
in Paris.

5. Hồ Chí Minh (Nguyễn Ái Quốc) to Sarraut, 7 September
1919; adjusted from the translation in Duiker, *Ho Chi
Minh*, p 61.

6. See his memoir *Une histoire de conspirateurs annamites à
Paris* (1928).

7. Quinn-Judge, *Ho Chi Minh*, p 18.

8. Pierre Brocheux, *Ho Chi Minh: a biography* (Cambridge
University Press, Cambridge: 2007) p 13.

9. Hue-Tam Ho Tai, *Radicalism and the Origins of the
Vietnamese Revolution* (Harvard University Press,
Harvard: 1992) p 69; cf. Thu Trang, *Hồ Chí Minh à Paris*,
pp 83–7.

10. Report of 30 January 1920; longer quotation in Thu
Trang, *Hồ Chí Minh à Paris*, pp 105–6. At that time Sean
T O'Kelly was using the Irish spelling Ó Ceallaigh. The
variant O'Callaigh, as in Lam's report, is found at least
once elsewhere, in a *New York Times* article (4 June 1920),
on O'Kelly's 1920 visit to Rome.

11. Lam's summary of 28 November 1919; longer quotation in
Thu Trang, *Hồ Chí Minh à Paris*, pp 82–3.

12. 'Indochine et Corée: une comparaison interessante' in *Le
Populaire* (4 September 1919); 'La question des indigènes
en Indochine' ['The native question in Indochina'] in
L'humanité (2 August 1919).

13. It did not happen, and the book is lost; it was not the
text eventually published as *Le procès de la colonisation
française* (1925). See Thu Trang, *Hồ Chí Minh à Paris*, pp
94–100.

14. Report of 12 October 1920 to Sarraut; full quotation in Thu Trang, *Hồ Chí Minh à Paris*, pp 107–11.
15. John Riddell (ed), *Founding the Communist International* (Anchor Foundation, New York: 1987) Vol 1, p 227.
16. The Lenoult motion at the party's National Council, 7 July 1919; full quotation in Thu Trang, *Hồ Chí Minh à Paris*, pp 90–1.
17. Hồ Chí Minh, 'Moi put' k Leninizmu' in *Problemy vostokovedeniya* (1960 no. 2) pp 19–20; Quinn-Judge, *Ho Chi Minh*, p 31.

1 Sources of South East Asian Nationhood

1. João de Barros, *Décadas da Asia* 2nd decade (Lisbon: 1553) Book 4 Chapter 3–4.
2. Miguel López de Gegazpi, 'Letter on his voyage to Cebu, 1565' in *Cartas al Rey Don Felipe II* as translated in Emma H Blair and James A Robertson, *The Philippine Islands 1493–1898* (A H Clark, Cleveland: 1903) Vol 2, p 196.
3. 'Account of the conquest of Manila, 1570' in *Cartas al Rey Don Felipe II* as translated in Blair and Robertson, *The Philippine Islands 1493–1898*, Vol 3, p 73.
4. 'Account of the conquest of Luzon, 1572' in *Cartas al Rey Don Felipe II* as translated in Blair and Robertson, *The Philippine Islands 1493–1898*, Vol 3, p 141.
5. J G Scott in *St James's Gazette* (1885) quoted in G E Mitton, *Scott of the Shan Hills* (John Murray, London: 1936) p 56.
6. D M Smeaton, *The Loyal Karens of Burma* (Kegan Paul, London: 1887) p 3.
7. Swapna Bhattacharya, 'A Close View of Encounter between British Burma and British Bengal': www.sasnet. lu.se/EASASpapers/19SwapnaBhattacharya.pdf.

8. Text of 16 May 1898; longer quotation and discussion in Worcester, *Philippines Past and Present* (Macmillan, New York: 1914) Vol 1, pp 22–4.

2 The Voice of Young Burma, 1906–22

1. U Maung Maung, *From Sangha to Laity: nationalist movements of Burma 1920–1940* (Manohar, New Delhi: 1980) p 1.

2. As reported in *Rangoon Gazette* (10 August 1908), reprinted in J S Furnivall, 'The Dawn of Nationalism in Burma' in *Journal of the Burma Research Society* Vol 33 (1950) pp 1–7.

3. *Report of the Police Administration* (Rangoon: 1919) p 11 as quoted in J F Cady, *A History of Modern Burma (Cornell University Press, Ithaca: 1958)* p 189, hereafter Cady, *History*.

4. *Report of the Committee Appointed to Ascertain and Advise how the Imperial Idea may be Inculcated and Fostered in Schools and Colleges in Burma* (Rangoon, 1917); Cady, *History*, pp 193–9.

5. *Parliamentary Debates, House of Commons* (20 August 1917).

6. San C Po, *Burma and the Karens* (Elliot Stock, London: 1928) Chapter 10.

7. Edwin Montagu, *An Indian Diary* (Heinemann, London: 1930) p 86; quoted in Hugh Tinker, *The Union of Burma* 4th ed. (Oxford University Press, London: 1967) p 2 n 3.

8. My narrative of this episode is based on Maung Maung, *From Sangha to Laity*, pp. 7–8 and notes. Dr Maung Maung (a different person) tells the story otherwise in his memoir 'U Thein Maung, Chief Justice of the Union', in Robert H Taylor (ed), *Dr. Maung Maung: Gentleman,*

Scholar, Patriot (Institute of Southeast Asian Studies,
Singapore: 2008) pp 158–70.

9. *Joint Report on Constitutional Reforms* (Montagu-
Chelmsford Report). Cd. 9109 (1918); all three quotations
from p 162.

10. *Annual Report on the Administration of Burma, 1918–1919*
(1919) p vii.

11. 'The Young Party … with difficulty raised some £2000
and despatched three representatives to London' (Sir
Reginald Craddock, *The Dilemma in India* [Constable,
London: 1929] p 116). There was no earlier published
source for the amount; the fact that Craddock specifies
it in his memoir strongly suggests that he benefited from
intelligence reports at the time when the mission was
being prepared.

12. *The Times* (14 August 1919) p 9; (20 August 1919) p 6.
Presumably an original title 'Paid emissaries in London
from Burma' was carelessly abridged by a sub-editor.

13. Craddock to Chelmsford, 4 September 1919, quoted in
Surendra Prasad Singh, *Growth of Nationalism in Burma
1900–1942* (Firma KLM, Calcutta: 1980) p 39.

14. Craddock to Chelmsford, 10 January 1920, quoted (from
the Montagu papers) in Surendra Prasad Singh, *Growth of
Nationalism in Burma*, p 46.

15. *The Times* (20 November 1919) p 15, leader.

16. Craddock, *The Dilemma in India*, pp 116–17.

17. *Hansard* (House of Commons, 4 December 1919).

18. *Burma Reforms Scheme.* Cmd. 746 (1920) p 30.

19. Reforms Department, Public Reforms Part B, *Proceedings*
nos. 320/322 (1920), quoted in Surendra Prasad Singh,
Growth of Nationalism in Burma, pp 42, 44.

20. For the dates see Aye Kyaw, *The Voice of Young Burma* (SEAP Publications, Singapore: 1993) pp 18–19.
21. Quoted by Aye Kyaw, *The Voice of Young Burma*, p 26.
22. In February 1921, according to Craddock, *The Dilemma in India*, p 119; not before December according to *Hansard* (House of Commons, 16 December 1921).
23. *The Times* (24 May 1921) p xiv; Aye Kyaw, *The Voice of Young Burma*, pp 21, 33.
24. *Annual report on the administration of Burma, 1920–1921* (1921).
25. Aye Kyaw, *The Voice of Young Burma*, pp. 44–5; Swapna Bhattacharya, 'A Close View of Encounter between British Burma and British Bengal': www.sasnet.lu.se/EASASpaper s/19SwapnaBhattacharya.pdf.
26. Craddock, *The Dilemma in India*, p 119.
27. Craddock, *The Dilemma in India*, pp 119–20.

3 What the Filipinos Ask, 1907–21

1. Program of the Nationalist Party, 12 March 1907; full quotation in Maximo M Kalaw, *Development of Philippine Politics* (Oriental Commercial Co., Manila: 1927) pp 304–6.
2. Quoted in Resil B Mojares, *The War Against the Americans: resistance and collaboration in Cebu, 1899–1906* (Ateneo de Manila University Press, Manila: 1999) pp 197–8.
3. Harry Bandholtz to Ralph H van Deman, 21 August 1907, quoted in Michael Cullinane, *Ilustrado Politics: Filipino elite responses to American rule, 1898–1908* (Ateneo de Manila University Press, Manila: 2003) pp 322–3. On the turnout see Kalaw, *Development of Philippine Politics*, pp 309–10.

4. Rafael Palma, *Nuestra compaña por la independencia desde Taft hasta Harrison (1901–1921)* (Manila: 1923), as translated in Cullinane, *Ilustrado Politics*, p 321.

5. *El Nuevo Dia* (16 April 1900), quoted in Mojares, *The War Against the Americans*, p 195.

6. Quezon's date of birth is conventionally given as 1878; for 1877 see www.pangulo.ph/prexy_mlq.php. 'Little Quezon' is from correspondence by an American administrator, James Harbord, who observed Osmeña's campaign in 1906; quoted in Cullinane, *Ilustrado Politics*, p 190. 'Frail and slender' Osmeña is from Rafael Palma, *Nuestra compaña por la independencia*, p 25; quoted in Kalaw, *Development of Philippine Politics*, p 312.

7. There is frequent discussion of this point in Francis B Harrison, *Origins of the Philippine Republic* (Department of Asian Studies, Cornell University, Ithaca: 1974).

8. Forbes to Taft, 13 November 1909, quoted in Cullinane, *Ilustrado Politics*, p 328.

9. Speech of 19 June 1908; fuller quotation in Kalaw, *Development of Philippine Politics*, pp 313–14.

10. George A Malcolm, *The Commonwealth of the Philippines* (Appleton-Century, New York: 1936) p 77.

11. Kalaw, *Development of Philippine Politics*, p 317.

12. Charles Elliott, *The Philippines to the End of the Commission Government* (1917) p 125.

13. Kalaw, *Development of Philippine Politics*, p 317.

14. Dr F S Watson reported in the *New York Times* (22 June 1912).

15. Francis B Harrison, *The Corner-Stone of Philippine Independence* (Century, New York: 1922) p 3; Harrison, *Origins of the Philippine Republic*, pp 212–13; cf. Kalaw, *Development of Philippine Politics*, pp 334, 352.

16. *New York Times* (27 December 1906); Harrison, *Origins of the Philippine Republic*, p 119 with Onorato's footnote.

17. Malcolm, *The Commonwealth of the Philippines*, p 80.

18. Speech of 6 October 1913; longer quotation in Harrison, *Origins of the Philippine Republic*, p x.

19. *New York Times* (28 December 1914).

20. See Harrison, *Origins of the Philippine Republic*, p 93 with Onorato's footnote.

21. Wilson to Harrison, 6 March 1915; longer quotation in Kalaw, *Development of Philippine Politics*, p 340.

22. Debate of 18 August 1916, quoted in Kalaw, *Development of Philippine Politics*, p 362.

23. *The Filipino People* Vol 2 No 11 (July 1914), quoted in Kalaw, *Development of Philippine Politics*, p 338.

24. Yeater to Baker, 15 February 1919; longer quotation in Honesto A Villanueva, 'The Independence Mission 1919: Independence Lies Ahead,' *Asian Studies* Vol 9 (1971) p 289.

25. Wilson to Baker, 3 March 1919; longer quotation in Villanueva, 'The Independence Mission 1919', p 293.

26. *Hearings before the Committee on the Philippines* (1919) pp 9, 14.

27. From Tom Fraser, *Chaim Weizmann: The Zionist Dream* (Haus Publishing, London: 2009), p. 76.

28. A S Link (ed), *The Papers of Woodrow Wilson,* Vol 59 (Princeton, NJ: 1988) p 204, Vol 60 (Princeton, NJ: 1989) pp 198–201.

29. Baker to Garrett, 8 June 1919; longer quotation in Villanueva, 'The Independence Mission 1919', pp 302–3.

30. 7 December 1920 (*Congressional Record*, 66th congress, 3rd session, 26); longer quotation in Villanueva, 'The Independence Mission 1919', p 304.

4 National and Colonial Questions: Indonesia, 1908–27

1. Full translation at marxists.anu.edu.au/archive/lenin/ works/1920/jul/x03.htm.

2. Semaun, 'An Early Account of the Independence Movement' in *Indonesia* No 1 (April 1966) p 52.

3. Leslie Palmier, *Communists in Indonesia* (Weidenfeld and Nicolson, London: 1973) p 16.

4. Deliar Noer, *The Modernist Muslim Movement in Indonesia, 1900–1942* (Oxford University Press, Singapore: 1973) p 108.

5. Tjokroaminoto in *Utusan Hindia* (7 and 24 March 1912); longer translations in Noer, *The Modernist Muslim Movement in Indonesia*, pp 111–12.

6. *M. N. Roy's Memoirs* (Allied Publishers, Bombay: 1964) p 383.

7. Noer, *The Modernist Muslim Movement in Indonesia*, p 122.

8. John Ingleson, *In Search of Justice: workers and unions in colonial Java, 1908–1926* (Oxford University Press, Singapore: 1986) p 105.

9. R E Elson, *The Idea of Indonesia: a history* (Cambridge University Press, Cambridge: 2008) p 33.

10. Condensed translation; full translation at marxists.anu. edu.au/archive/lenin/works/1920/jun/05.htm.

11. Quinn-Judge, *Ho Chi Minh*, p 49.

12. Debate of 26 July 1920; full translation in John Riddell (ed), *Workers of the World and Oppressed Peoples, Unite!* (Pathfinder Press, New York: 1991) Vol 1, p 158; cf. Ruth McVey, *The Rise of Indonesian Communism* (Cornell University Press, Ithaca: 1965) pp 55–61.

13. Sneevliet used 'Mecca' as a codeword for Moscow in his correspondence: see Tony Saich, *The Origins of the First*

United Front in China: the role of Sneevliet (alias Maring) (Brill, Leiden: 1991) Vol 1, p 280.

14. Noer, *The Modernist Muslim Movement in Indonesia*, p 123.

15. 'Leven en dood van een revolutionair' in *De Tribune* (29 March 1952).

16. McVey, *The Rise of Indonesian Communism*, pp 34–5.

17. Elson, *The Idea of Indonesia: a history*, p 45.

18. Report of 1 June 1923; longer translation in John Ingleson, 'Bound Hand and Foot: railway workers and the 1923 strike in Java' in *Indonesia* No 31 (1981) p 71.

19. Tan Malaka, *Naar de 'Republiek Indonesia'* (1925) pp 21, 23; these and further quotations in Elson, *The Idea of Indonesia: a history*, pp 50–8.

20. Quinn-Judge, *Ho Chi Minh*, pp 94–5.

21. McVey, *The Rise of Indonesian Communism*, p 346.

5 Demands of the Vietnamese People, 1906–26

1. Full text (translated by Edouard Huber) in *Bulletin de l'Ecole Française d'Extrême-Orient* Vol 7 (1907) pp 166–75. See William Duiker, *The Rise of Nationalism in Vietnam, 1900–1941* (Cornell University Press, Ithaca: 1976) pp 54–5; David Marr, *Vietnamese Anticolonialism 1885–1925* (University of California Press, Berkeley: 1971) pp 159–63.

2. Phan Bội Châu, *Việt Nam vong quốc sử* (1905); *Hải ngoại huyết thư* (1906). See Marr, *Vietnamese Anticolonialism 1885–1925*, pp 114–23, 128–31.

3. Marr, *Vietnamese Anticolonialism 1885–1925*, pp 163–82; Morlat, *Les affaires politiques de l'Indochine 1895–1923*, p 87.

4. Beau's annual report to the Colonial Minister, 1907; longer quota'ion in Trinh Van Thao, *L'école française en Indochine* (Karthala, Paris: 1995) p 50.

5. Duiker, *Ho Chi Minh*, pp 36–7 and note 19.

6. Morlat, *Les affaires politiques de l'Indochine 1895–1923*, pp 81–8; Marr, *Vietnamese Anticolonialism 1885–1925*, pp 193–5; Claude Gendre, *Le Dê Thám (1858–1913) un résistant vietnamien à la colonisation française* (L'Harmattan, Paris: 2007) pp 101–5.

7. See Jonathan Clements, *Wellington Koo: China* (Haus Publishing, London: 2008) p 30.

8. Marr, *Vietnamese Anticolonialism 1885–1925*, p 220 and note 27; Phan-văn-Trường, *Une histoire de conspirateurs annamites à Paris* (Giadinh [i.e. Saigon]: 1928; new ed. by Ngo Van Xuyet: L'Insomniaque, Montreuil: 2003) pp 99–104.

9. Inukai Tsuyoshi to Cường Để, 1916; translation adjusted from Trần Mỹ-Vân, *A Vietnamese Royal Exile in Japan: Prince Cường Để (1882–1951)* (Routledge, London: 2005) p 97.

10. Phan Chu Trinh, 'Les manifestations annamites de 1908' in *Bulletin officiel de la Ligue des Droits de l'Homme* No 20 (31 October 1912) pp 1161–2, as translated in Marr, *Vietnamese Anticolonialism 1885–1925*, p 245.

11. To Anna Louise Strong, quoted in Duiker, *Ho Chi Minh*, p 45.

12. Nguyễn Tất Thành to President of the Republic, 15 September 1911, www.hungviet.org/hcm/xinhoc.html; full translation, Duiker, *Ho Chi Minh*, pp 47–8.

13. Quinn-Judge, *Ho Chi Minh*, p 24.

14. Both quotations from Trần Mỹ-Vân, *A Vietnamese Royal Exile in Japan*, pp 100–1 (translations adjusted).

15. Phan Chu Trinh to Nguyễn Ái Quốc, 18 February 1922. Longer quotation in English in Quinn-Judge, *Ho Chi Minh*, p 38; full quotation in French in Thu Trang, *Hồ Chí Minh à Paris*, pp 181–7.
16. Thu Trang, *Hồ Chí Minh à Paris*, p 187.
17. The correspondence was in fact quoted in Parliament in the colonial budget debate in February 1925; full quotation in French in Phan-văn-Trường, *Une histoire de conspirateurs annamites à Paris*, pp 208–23.
18. Quinn-Judge, *Ho Chi Minh*, pp 54–5.
19. Debate of 20 June 1924; full translation in *International Press Correspondence [Inprecor]* No 41 (16 July 1924) p 405.
20. Debate of 1 July 1924; fuller translation in Quinn-Judge, *Ho Chi Minh*, pp 56–7.
21. ROSTA, a precursor of TASS. Quinn-Judge, *Ho Chi Minh*, p 66.
22. Quinn-Judge, *Ho Chi Minh*, p 83.

6 Siam Reasserts Independence, 1917–39

1. *The Times* (24 April 1917) p 8.
2. David K Wyatt, *The Politics of Reform in Thailand* (Yale University Press, New Haven: 1969) pp 89–91; Chula Chakrabongse, *Lords of Life: the paternal monarchy of Bangkok 1782–1932* (Alvin Redman, London: 1960) pp 261–3.
3. All quotations from Bernard M Allen, *Sir Robert Morant: a great public servant* (Macmillan, London: 1934) pp 49–50.
4. Arnold Wright and Oliver Brakspear, *Twentieth Century Impressions of Siam* (Lloyd's, London: 1908) p 154; aquitailandia.blogspot.com/2007_08_01_archive.html

5. Reported in Jusserand (French ambassador in Washington) to Lansing (Secretary of State), 12 September 1919, as summarised in Victor Purcell, 'The Relinquishment by the United States of Extraterritoriality in Siam' in *Journal of the Royal Asiatic Society, Malayan Branch* Vol 37 (1964) p 117.

6. Morlat, *Les affaires politiques de l'Indochine 1895–1923*, pp 291–3.

7. Charoon to Vajiravudh, quoted in Walter F Vella, *Chaiyo! King Vajiravudh and the Development of Thai Nationalism* (University of Hawaii Press, Honolulu: 1978) p 122.

8. Wilson to Polk, 27 February 1920, with reply 28 February, in Link (ed), *The Papers of Woodrow Wilson* Vol 64, p 479, Vol 65, p 21; quoted in Purcell, 'The Relinquishment by the United States of Extraterritoriality in Siam', pp 99–120.

9. For the change see Purcell, 'The Relinquishment by the United States of Extraterritoriality in Siam', pp 106 and 118; Francis B Sayre, 'The Passing of Extraterritoriality in Siam' in *American Journal of International Law* Vol 22 (1928) pp 70–88, esp. p 81.

10. Sayre to Vajiravudh, quoted in Francis B Sayre, *Glad Adventure* (Macmillan, New York: 1957) p 122. Cf. Vella, *Chaiyo! King Vajiravudh and the Development of Thai Nationalism*, p 124.

11. Scot Barmé, *Luang Wichit Wathakan and the Creation of a Thai Identity* (Institute of Southeast Asian Studies, Singapore: 1993) p 42.

12. For the dates of the new treaties see Sayre, 'The Passing of Extraterritoriality in Siam', p 87.

13. *The Times* (London, 10 May 1927) p 15.

14. Benjamin A Batson, *The End of the Absolute Monarchy in Siam* (Oxford University Press, New York: 1984) p 80.

15. Judith A Stowe, *Siam Becomes Thailand: a story of intrigue* (Hurst, London: 1991) p 10.

16. Batson, *The End of the Absolute Monarchy in Siam*, p 79 (translation slightly adjusted).

17. Stowe, *Siam Becomes Thailand*, pp. 11–12; Walter F Vella, 'The Impact of the West on Government in Thailand' in *University of California Publications in Political Science* Vol 4 (1955) pp 317–410, esp pp 363–4.

18. *The Times* (London, 30 May 1929) p 7.

19. Ultimatum and Prajadhipok's reply, 24 June 1932, quoted in Roger M Smith (ed), *Southeast Asia: documents of political development and change* (Cornell University Press, Ithaca: 1974) p 26; K P Landon, *Siam in Transition* (Greenwood Press, New York: 1939) p 10; Chula Chakrabongse, *Lords of Life*, pp 313–14.

20. Letter to Prince Chula Chakrabongse, January 1933, quoted in his *Lords of Life*, p 316.

7 From Resistance to Independence in South East Asia

1. Quoted in David Kenley, *New Culture in a New World: the May Fourth Movement and the Chinese diaspora in Singapore 1919–1932* (Routledge, London: 2003) p 50.

2. C F Yong and R B McKenna, 'Sir Arthur Young and Political Control of the Chinese in Singapore, 1911–1919' in *Journal of the Malaysian Branch of the Royal Asiatic Society* Vol 57, part 2 (1984) pp 1–30.

3. For the full story see C F Yong and R B McKenna, *The Kuomintang Movement in British Malaya 1912–1949* (Singapore University Press, Singapore: 1990) pp 22–82; note also Yeo Kim Wah, 'The Guillemard-Maxwell Power Struggle, 1921–1925' in *Journal of the Malaysian Branch of the Royal Asiatic Society* Vol 54, part 1 (1981) pp 48–64.

4. Maria Pilar S Luna, 'General Artemio Ricarte y Garcia, a Filipino nationalist' in *Asian Studies* Vol 9 (1971) pp 229–41; Harrison, *Origins of the Philippine Republic*, pp 17, 161 with Onorato's footnotes; Harrison, *The Corner-Stone of Philippine Independence*, pp 151–2.

5. See http://www.lakorn.org/btf2003/buildings_eng.php.

6. Elson, *The Idea of Indonesia: a history*, p 141.

7. On this period see Harrison, *Origins of the Philippine Republic*.

8. G E R Grant Brown, *Burma As I Saw It* (Stokes, New York: 1925) p 172.

9. John Buchan, *The Three Hostages* (Hodder & Stoughton, London: 1924) Chapter 13.

Chronology

YEAR	COUNTRY	THE LIVES AND THE LANDS
1905	Philippines	22 Aug: Osmeña presents memorial on independence to William Taft, US Secretary of War.
1906	Burma	YMBA founded by Ba Pe, Maung Gyi and Hla Pe.
	Indochina	Jan: Prince Cường Để leaves Huế secretly for Japan.
		Aug: Phan Chu Trinh presents memorial on the destruction of Vietnamese culture to the Governor-General of Indochina.
1907	Indochina	'Eastern Capital Free School' opens briefly.
	Philippines	12 Mar: Nacionalista Party founded, advocating independence.
		30 Jul: First elections for Assembly; widespread gains for Nacionalista Party.
1908	Dutch Indies	20 May: Budi Utomo, Islamic organisation, founded.
	Indochina	27 Jun: Attempted poisoning of French garrison at Hanoi; activists arrested and deported, courts suspended.
	Burma	Aug: May Oung speaks on 'The modern Burman: his life and notions'.
1909	Indochina	Oct: Prince Cường Để expelled from Japan: he and Phan Bội Châu find refuge in Siam.
	Philippines	2 Nov: Second elections for Assembly.

YEAR	HISTORY	CULTURE
1905	Japanese victorious in Russo-Japanese War.	E M Forster, *Where Angels Fear to Tread*.
1906	Edward VII of England and Kaiser Wilhelm II of Germany meet.	Nobel Prize in Literature: Giosue Carducci (Italy).
	Major earthquake in San Francisco USA kills over 1,000.	John Galsworthy, *A Man of Property*.
		Jules Massenet, *Ariane*.
1907	New Zealand granted Dominion status.	Nobel Prize in Literature: Rudyard Kipling (Great Britain).
	Grigory Rasputin gains influence at the court of Tsar Nicholas II.	Pablo Picasso, *Les Demoiselles d'Avignon*.
	Peace Conference held in The Hague.	
1908	*The Daily Telegraph* publishes German Kaiser Wilhelm II's hostile remarks towards England.	Nobel Prize in Literature: Rudolf Eucken (Germany).
	Union of South Africa established.	Kenneth Grahame, *The Wind in the Willows*.
	Britain's Edward VII and Russia's Tsar meet at Reval.	Bela Bartok, *String Quartet No.1*.
	William Howard Taft elected US President.	Edward Elgar, *Symphony No. 1 in A-Flat*.
1909	Anglo-German discussions on control of Baghdad railway.	Nobel Prize in Literature: Selma Lagerlöf (Sweden).
	Turkish nationalists force Kiamil Pasha, Grand Vizier of Turkey, to resign.	H G Wells, *Tono-Bungay*.
	Plastic (Bakelite) invented.	Vasily Kandinsky paints first abstract paintings.

YEAR	COUNTRY	THE LIVES AND THE LANDS
1910	Philippines	14 May: Manuel Quezon's maiden speech before US House of Representatives.
	Siam	23 Oct: King Chulalongkorn dies and is succeeded by Vajiravudh.
1911	Indochina	1 Jun: Albert Sarraut appointed Governor-General.
		2 Jun: Nguyễn Tất Thành (Hồ Chí Minh) goes to sea.
1912	Dutch Indies	10 Sep: Sarekat Islam founded by Samanhudi.
		25 Dec: Indische Partij founded by Douwes Dekker.
1913	Siam	Prince Traidos appointed deputy foreign minister.
		Prince Charoon is minister (ambassador) in Paris.
	Philippines	6 Oct: Francis Burton Harrison's inaugural address as Governor-General, promising rapid progress towards self-government.
1914	Dutch Indies	9 May: ISDV founded by Henk Sneevliet.

YEAR	HISTORY	CULTURE
1910	Britain's King Edward VII dies; succeeded by George V. Liberals win British General Election. South Africa becomes Dominion within British Empire with Louis Botha as Premier.	Nobel Prize in Literature: Paul von Heyse (Germany). Karl May, *Winnetou*. Edward Elgar, *Concerto for Violin in B Minor, Op. 61*. R Vaughan Williams, *Sea Symphony*.
1911	US-Japanese and Anglo-Japanese commercial treaties signed. German gunboat *Panther* arrives in Agadir: triggers international crisis.	Nobel Prize in Literature: Maurice Maeterlinck (Belgium). D H Lawrence, *The White Peacock*. Richard Strauss, *Der Rosenkavalier*.
1912	*Titanic* sinks: 1,513 die. First Balkan War begins. Woodrow Wilson elected US President.	C G Jung, *The Theory of Psychoanalysis*. Marc Chagall, *The Cattle Dealer*. Maurice Ravel, *Daphnis et Chloé*.
1913	London Ambassadors Conference ends First Balkan War: establishes independent Albania. Second Balkan War begins and ends. Mahatma Gandhi, leader of Indian Passive Resistance Movement, arrested.	Nobel Prize in Literature: Sir R Tagore (India). Thomas Mann, *Death in Venice*. Marcel Proust, *Du côté de chez Swann*. Grand Central Station in New York completed.
1914	Outbreak of First World War.	Gustav Holst, *The Planets*.

YEAR	COUNTRY	· THE LIVES AND THE LANDS
1916	Siam	Patriarch Vajirañana publishes 'The Buddhist attitude towards national defence and administration' arguing that Buddhists can fight in a just war.
	Dutch Indies	21 Mar: J P van Limburg Stirum takes office as Governor-General.
	Philippines	29 Aug: Philippine Autonomy Act ('Jones Law') passed by US Congress.
	Indochina	7 Nov: Albert Sarraut appointed to second term as Governor-General of Indochina (takes office January 1917).
1917	Siam	22 Jul: Siam enters the First World War.
	Burma	20 Aug: Edwin Montagu states in British Parliament that home rule is the ultimate aim for India (including, by implication, Burma).
		Nov: Burmese delegation meets Montagu in India to urge separation from India and self-government.
1918	Dutch Indies	First elections for Volksraad.
	Burma	15 Feb: Reginald Craddock takes office as Lieutenant-Governor.
	Siam	Feb: Siamese-French treaty renegotiations begin in Bangkok.
		Aug: Siamese troops reach Marseilles to participate in final months of First World War.
	Dutch Indies	Dec: Henk Sneevliet expelled after he promotes uprising in the army.

YEAR	HISTORY	CULTURE
1916	First World War: Battles of Verdun, the Somme and Jutland. US President Woodrow Wilson re-elected. Wilson issues Peace Note to belligerents in European war. David Lloyd George becomes British Prime Minister.	Nobel Prize in Literature: V von Heidenstam (Sweden). Henri Matisse, *The Three Sisters*. Claude Monet, *Waterlilies*. 'Dada' movement produces iconoclastic 'anti-art'. Richard Strauss, *Ariadne auf Naxos*. Film: *Intolerance*.
1917	First World War: Battle of Passchendaele (Third Ypres); USA declares war on Germany; China declares war on Germany and Russia. February Revolution in Russia. German and Russian delegates sign armistice at Brest-Litovsk.	P G Wodehouse, *The Man With Two Left Feet*. T S Eliot, *Prufrock and Other Observations*. Sergei Prokofiev, *Classical Symphony*. Film: *Easy Street*.
1918	First World War: Peace Treaty of Brest-Litovsk signed between Russia and Central Powers; German Spring offensives on Western Front fail; Romania signs Peace of Bucharest with Germany and Austria-Hungary; Allied offensives on Western Front have German army in full retreat; Armistice signed between Allies and Germany.	Alexander Blok, *The Twelve*. Gerard Manley Hopkins, *Poems*. Luigi Pirandello, *Six Characters in Search of an Author*. Bela Bartok, *Bluebeard's Castle*. Giacomo Puccini, *Il Trittico*. Gustav Cassel, *Theory of Social Economy*. Edvard Munch, *Bathing Man*.

YEAR	COUNTRY	THE LIVES AND THE LANDS
1919	Siam	18 Jan: Paris Peace Conference begins; Charoon, Traidos and Phya Bibadh Kosha represent Siam.
	Indochina	12 Feb: Prince Cường Để, in Japan, appeals to President Wilson and the Paris Peace Conference for Vietnamese independence.
	Philippines	28 Feb: Independence Mission leaves Manila for Washington.
	Indochina	May: Albert Sarraut leaves Hanoi for Paris.
		18 Jun: Hồ Chí Minh addresses 'Claims of the Vietnamese People' to Georges Clemenceau and Paris Peace Conference.
	Singapore	19 Jun: Rioting in Singapore in protest at Paris Peace Conference decision against China on Shandong.
	Philippines	28 June: Independence Mission in Washington addresses House and Senate Committee on Insular Affairs.
	Burma	7 Jul: Home Rule Delegation leaves Rangoon for London, headed by Ba Pe; holds talks with Montagu and addresses Parliamentary Select Committee.
	Indochina	6 Sep: Albert Sarraut interviews Hồ Chí Minh in Paris.
	Siam	18 Dec: Siam and US sign revised treaty.

YEAR	HISTORY	CULTURE
1919	Communist Revolt in Berlin.	Nobel Prize in Literature: Carl Spitteler (Switzerland).
	2–6 Mar: Communist International (Comintern) founded in Moscow.	Bauhaus movement founded by Walter Gropius.
	Benito Mussolini founds Fascist movement in Italy.	Wassily Kandinsky, *Dreamy Improvisation*.
	Britain and France authorise resumption of commercial relations with Germany.	Paul Klee, *Dream Birds*.
		Thomas Hardy, *Collected Poems*.
		Herman Hesse, *Demian*.
	British-Persian agreement at Tehran to preserve integrity of Persia.	George Bernard Shaw, *Heartbreak House*.
	Irish War of Independence begins.	Edward Elgar, *Concerto in E Minor for Cello*.
	US Senate vetoes ratification of Versailles Treaty leaving US outside League of Nations.	Manuel de Falla, *The Three-Cornered Hat*.
		Film: *The Cabinet of Dr Caligari*.

YEAR	COUNTRY	THE LIVES AND THE LANDS
1920	Dutch Indies	May: Asser Baars founds PKI as a reincarnation of the ISDV; Semaun is its first chairman.
		5 Jun: Lenin's 'Theses on National and Colonial Questions' circulated in advance of Comintern congress.
	Siam	13 Jun: Chakrabongse, likely successor to the throne, dies of Spanish flu.
	Dutch Indies	19 Jul: Second Comintern Congress opens in Moscow; Henk Sneevliet speaks for Dutch Indies and is secretary of National and Colonial Commission; Congress approves working with revolutionary nationalist movements in the East
	Siam	Nov: Prince Charoon is Siamese delegate at first League of Nations General Assembly.
	Burma	Nov: First Legislative Council elections. Ba Pe's Twenty One Party wins majority.
	Dutch Indies and Indochina	Dec: PKI affiliates to Comintern; in the same month, at its Congress at Tours attended by Hồ Chí Minh, French Socialist Party affiliates to Comintern.
	Burma	5 Dec: Boycott of University of Rangoon begins.

YEAR	HISTORY	CULTURE
1920	Apr: Grigory Voitinsky begins Comintern mission in China.	Nobel Prize in Literature: Knut Hamsun (Norway).
	League of Nations comes into existence.	F Scott Fitzgerald, *This Side of Paradise*.
	The Hague selected as seat of International Court of Justice.	Franz Kafka, *The Country Doctor*.
		Katherine Mansfield, *Bliss*.
	League of Nations headquarters moves to Geneva.	Rambert School of Ballet formed in London.
	Warren G Harding wins US Presidential election.	Lyonel Feininger, *Church*.
	Bolsheviks win Russian Civil War.	Juan Gris, *Book and Newspaper*.
	Government of Ireland Act passed.	Vincent D'Indy, *The Legend Of St Christopher*.
	Adolf Hitler announces his 25-point programme in Munich.	Maurice Ravel, *La Valse*.

YEAR	COUNTRY	THE LIVES AND THE LANDS
1921	Philippines	Harrison ends term as governor-general of Philippines.
	Dutch Indies	Apr: Van Limburg Stirum replaced as Governor-General by Dirk Fock.
		May: Asser Baars leaves Dutch Indies.
		22 Jun: Third Comintern Congress opens in Moscow; Darsono represents PKI.
	Burma	July: Ottama's sentence of 10 months' imprisonment causes riots.
		5 Oct: Leonard Wood takes office as Governor-General; Forbes-Wood report advises time not ripe for independence.
		7 Oct: Edwin Montagu states in British Parliament that dyarchy is the aim for Burma.
		20 Oct: Ninth All Burma Conference of GCBA votes to boycott Burma Reforms Committee hearings and Prince of Wales' visit.
		2 Dec: Prince of Wales begins visit; Chit Hlaing arrested.
	Dutch Indies	Dec: Eighth Congress of PKI elects Tan Malaka as chairman.
1922	Dutch Indies	21 Jan: First Congress of the Workers of the East in Moscow; Semaun represents PKI.
		Mar: Tan Malaka expelled.
	Burma	Aug: GCBA and Twenty-One Party hold rival congresses.
		Nov: First elections under dyarchy; 7 per cent turnout.
	Dutch Indies	5 Nov: Fourth Comintern Congress opens in Moscow; Tan Malaka represents PKI.
	Burma	21 Dec: Reginald Craddock succeeded by Harcourt Butler, with title of governor from 2 January 1923. He selects first cabinet.

YEAR	HISTORY	CULTURE
1921	4 Mar: Warren Harding succeeds Woodrow Wilson as US President.	Nobel Prize in Literature: Anatole France (France).
	23 Jul: First Congress of Chinese Communist Party opens in Shanghai; Sneevliet represents Comintern.	Georges Braque, *Still Life with Guitar*.
		Max Ernst, *The Elephant Celebes*.
		Aldous Huxley, *Crome Yellow*.
	Irish Free State established.	D H Lawrence, *Women in Love*.
	Peace treaty signed between Russia and Germany.	John Dos Passos, *Three Soldiers*.
		Salzburg Festival established.
	State of Emergency proclaimed in Germany in face of economic crisis.	Arthur Honegger, *Le Roi David*.
		Sergei Prokofiev, *The Love for Three Oranges*.
	Washington Naval Treaty signed.	
1922	Chanak Crisis.	Nobel Prize in Literature: J Benevente y Martinez (Spain).
	Britain recognises Kingdom of Egypt under Fuad I.	T S Eliot, *The Waste Land*.
	Mahatma Gandhi sentenced to six years in prison for civil disobedience.	James Joyce, *Ulysses*.
		F Scott Fitzgerald, *The Beautiful and Damned*.
	Election in Irish Free State gives majority to Pro-Treaty candidates: IRA takes large areas under its control.	Hermann Hesse, *Siddhartha*.
		Max Beckmann, *Before the Bell*.
		Clive Bell, *Since Cezanne*.
	League of Nations Council approves British Mandate in Palestine.	Irving Berlin, *April Showers*.
		Film: *Dr. Mabuse the Gambler*.

YEAR	COUNTRY	THE LIVES AND THE LANDS
1923	Dutch Indies	17 Feb: Sarekat Islam becomes PSI, still led by Tjokroaminoto, and excludes communists.
	Indochina	Jun: Hồ Chí Minh leaves Paris for Moscow and reports to Comintern's Indonesia Commission.
	Dutch Indies	Aug: Semaun expelled after government clamps down on railway strike and detains activists.
	Indochina	15 Oct: Nguyễn An Ninh speaks on 'L'idéal de la jeunesse annamite'.
	Dutch Indies	Dec: Tan Malaka appointed Comintern representative for South East Asia at Guangzhou (Canton); Henk Sneevliet returns to the Netherlands and the Dutch communist movement.
	Indochina	11 Dec: Nguyễn An Ninh founds *La cloche fêlée*.
1924	Indochina	24 Jan: Lenin dies in Moscow; Hồ Chí Minh attends funeral.
	Burma	10 May: Eleventh All Burma Conference of GCBA.
	Indochina	19 Jun: Attempted assassination of Martial Merlin, Governor-General of French Indochina, at Guangzhou.
	Burma	Aug/Sep: Widespread disturbances; Ottama sentenced to three years' imprisonment.
	Indochina	Nov: Hồ Chí Minh arrives in Guangzhou.

YEAR	HISTORY	CULTURE
1923	French and Belgian troops occupy the Ruhr when Germany fails to make reparation payments. USSR formally comes into existence. Severe earthquake in Japan destroys all of Yokohama, most of Tokyo. Miguel Primo de Rivera assumes dictatorship of Spain. Wilhelm Marx succeeds Gustav Stresemann as German Chancellor. State of Emergency declared in Germany. British Mandate in Palestine begins. Adolf Hitler's *coup d'état* (Beer Hall Putsch) fails.	Nobel Prize in Literature: W B Yeats (Ireland). François Mauriac, *Genitrix*. P G Wodehouse, *The Inimitable Jeeves*. Edna St Vincent Millay, *The Ballad of the Harp-Weaver; A Few Figs from Thistles*. Martin Buber, *I and Thou*. Sigmund Freud, *The Ego and the Id*. Max Beckmann, *The Trapeze*. Mark Chagall, *Love Idyll*. George Gershwin, *Rhapsody in Blue*. Bela Bartok, *Dance Suite*. BBC listings magazine *Radio Times* first published.
1924	Dawes Plan published. Turkish National Assembly expels Ottoman dynasty. Greece proclaimed republic. Labour Party loses general election after *Daily Mail* publishes Zinoviev Letter. German Nazi Party enters Reichstag with 32 seats for first time after elections. Calvin Coolidge elected US President.	Nobel Prize in Literature: Wladyslaw S Reymot (Poland). Noel Coward, *The Vortex*. E M Forster, *A Passage to India*. Thomas Mann, *The Magic Mountain*. George Bernard Shaw, *St Joan*. 'The Blue Four' expressionist group is formed. Georges Braque, *Sugar Bowl*. Fernand Leger, *Ballet Mecanique*.

YEAR	COUNTRY	THE LIVES AND THE LANDS
1925	Siam	9 Feb: Asdang, King Vajiravudh's elder surviving brother and likely successor, dies.
	Indochina	May: Phan Chu Trinh returns from Paris.
		17 Jun: André Malraux founds *L'Indochine* (evading an attempted ban he soon refounds it as *L'Indochine enchaînée*).
		30 Jun: First meeting of League of Oppressed Peoples, Guangzhou.
		Jul: Phan Bội Châu is trapped by French agents in China and soon afterwards sentenced to death.
	Siam	Aug: Italy surrenders unequal rights in Siam, last of the treaty powers to do so.
	Indochina	Nov: Alexandre Varenne takes office as Governor-General; he reprieves Phan Bội Châu.
	Burma	Nov: Second elections; 16 per cent turnout.
	Siam	25 Nov: King Vajiravudh dies, naming Prajadhipok as his successor.
1926	Dutch Indies	Jan: Darsono expelled after widespread strikes fostered by communist unions.
	Indochina	24 Mar: Phan Chu Trinh dies; Nguyễn An Ninh arrested.
	Dutch Indies	Jun: Alimin and Musso appeal to Comintern for support for uprising in Dutch Indies.
		Nov: Abortive communist-led uprisings in Java and elsewhere.
		18 Dec: Alimin and Musso arrested in Johor (Malaya) on their return from Moscow.

YEAR	HISTORY	CULTURE
1925	Christiania, Norwegian capital, renamed Oslo.	Nobel Prize in Literature: George Bernard Shaw (Ireland).
	Mussolini announces he will take dictatorial powers in Italy.	Noel Coward, *Hay Fever*.
		Franz Kafka, *The Trial*.
	British Pound Sterling returns to Gold Standard.	Virginia Woolf, *Mrs Dalloway*.
		Pablo Picasso, *Three Dancers*.
	Paul von Hindenburg elected President of Germany.	Marc Chagall, *The Drinking Green Pig*.
	Hitler reorganises Nazi Party in Germany.	Lyonel Feininger, *Tower*.
	Locarno Treaty signed in London.	Alban Berg, *Wozzek*.
		Ferruccio Busconi, *Doctor Faust*.
		Film: *Battleship Potemkin*.
1926	General Strike in Britain.	Nobel Prize in Literature: Grazia Deledda (Italy).
	Germany applies for admission to League of Nations; blocked by Spain and Brazil.	A A Milne, *Winnie the Pooh*.
		Ernest Hemingway, *The Sun Also Rises*.
	France proclaims the Lebanon republic.	Sean O'Casey, *The Plough and The Stars*.
	Germany admitted to League of Nations; Spain leaves as result.	Oskar Kokoschka, *Terrace in Richmond*.
	Imperial Conference in London decides Britain and Dominions are autonomous communities, equal in status.	Edvard Munch, *The Red House*.
		Eugene D'Albert, *The Golem*.
		Giacomo Puccini, *Turandot*.
		Film: *The General*.

YEAR	COUNTRY	THE LIVES AND THE LANDS
1927	Indochina	Apr: Hồ Chí Minh escapes China, finding refuge in Soviet Union.
	Dutch Indies	4 Jul: Indonesian National Association founded; renamed Indonesian National Party in 1928.
1930	Indochina	10 Feb: Yên Bái mutiny and failed VNQDD uprising in Vietnam.
	Burma	22 Dec: Outbreak of Saya San rebellion.
1931	Burma	27 Nov: Burma Round Table Conference opens in London. Next day in Burma Saya San is executed.
1932	Siam	10 Dec: King Prajadhipok proclaims constitutional monarchy.
1933	Siam	Oct: Counter-coup fails; Bavoradej exiled.
1934	Philippines	24 Mar: After 12th Philippine Independence Mission the Tydings-McDuffie Act, providing for Commonwealth of the Philippines and for independence in 1946, becomes law in US.
		12 Oct: Francis Harrison, former governor, returns as political adviser to Manuel Quezon.

YEAR	HISTORY	CULTURE
1927	Inter-Allied military control of Germany ends. India Commission under Sir John Simon established to review Montagu-Chelmsford Act.	Virginia Woolf, *To the Lighthouse.* Adolf Hitler, *Mein Kampf.* Film: *The Jazz Singer.*
1930	Britain, France, Italy, Japan and US sign London Naval Treaty regulating naval expansion. British Imperial Conference held in London.	Nobel Prize in Literature: Sinclair Lewis (USA). W H Auden, *Poems.* Igor Stravinsky, *Symphony of Psalms.* Film: *All Quiet on the Western Front.*
1931	Delhi Pact between Viceroy of India and Mahatma Gandhi suspends civil disobedience campaign.	Robert Frost, *Collected Poems.* Salvador Dali, *The Persistence of Memory.* Film: *Little Caesar.*
1932	Franklin D Roosevelt wins US Presidential election.	Aldous Huxley, *Brave New World.* Film: *Grand Hotel.*
1933	Adolf Hitler appointed Chancellor of Germany. Japan announces it will leave League of Nations.	George Orwell, *Down and Out in Paris and London.* Duke Ellington's Orchestra debuts in Britain. Film: *King Kong.*
1934	Germany: 'Night of the Long Knives'; role of German President and Chancellor merged, Hitler becomes *Führer* after German President Paul von Hindenburg dies. Japan repudiates Washington Treaties of 1922 and 1930.	Nobel Prize in Literature: Luigi Pirandello (Italy). F Scott Fitzgerald, *Tender Is the Night.* Robert Graves, *I, Claudius.* Dmitri Shostakovich, *Lady Macbeth of Mtsensk.* Sergei Rakhmaninov, *Rhapsody on a Theme of Paganini.*

YEAR	COUNTRY	THE LIVES AND THE LANDS
1935	Siam	2 Mar: Prajadhipok abdicates; his successor is Ananda Mahidol, aged 9, who is at school in Switzerland.
	Philippines	15 Nov: Manuel Quezon takes office as President of Commonwealth of the Philippines.
1937	Burma	1 Apr: Burma, separated from India, becomes a British crown colony with a fully elected legislature; Ba Maw is first prime minister.
1938	Siam	16 Dec: Pibul becomes prime minister, a position he retains until August 1944. Siam is renamed Thailand in 1939.
1940	Indochina	Sep: Japan occupies Indochina (which remains under Vichy French administration).
	Thailand	Oct: Thailand invades Cambodia and Laos.

YEAR	HISTORY	CULTURE
1935	Anglo-Indian trade pact signed. British King George V's Silver Jubilee. Hoare-Laval Pact. League of Nations imposes sanctions against Italy following invasion of Abyssinia.	George Gershwin, *Porgy and Bess.* T S Eliot, *Murder in the Cathedral.* Emlyn Williams, *Night Must Fall.* Ivy Compton-Burnett, *A House and its Head.* Films: *The 39 Steps. Top Hat.*
1937	Japan invades China: captures Shanghai; Rape of Nanjing (250,000 Chinese killed). Britain's George VI crowned.	Fernand Leger, *Le Transport des Forces.* Pablo Picasso, *Guernica.* Jean-Paul Sartre, *Nausea.* Film: *Snow White and the Seven Dwarfs.*
1938	German troops enter Austria, declaring it part of German Reich. Japanese puppet government of China at Nanjing. Munich Agreement hands Sudetenland to Germany.	Nobel Prize in Literature: Pearl Buck (USA). Evelyn Waugh, *Scoop.* Films: *Pygmalion. Alexander Nevsky. The Adventures of Robin Hood.*
1940	Second World War: Germany invades Holland, Belgium, Luxembourg and France. France divides into German-occupied north and Vichy south.	Ernest Hemingway, *For Whom the Bell Tolls.* Eugene O'Neill, *Long Days Journey into Night.* Films: *The Great Dictator. Pinocchio. Rebecca.*

YEAR	COUNTRY	THE LIVES AND THE LANDS
1941	Indochina	Feb: Hồ Chí Minh crosses border from China and begins armed resistance.
	Philippines	8 Dec: Japan attacks Philippines.
	Thailand	21 Dec: Japan and Thailand sign military alliance; already occupying strategic positions in Thailand, Japan rapidly attacks Malaya, Burma and Dutch Indies.
1942	Burma	15 Feb: Japan captures Singapore; Japanese invade Burma.
	Philippines	8 May: US surrender of Philippines to Japan.
1944	Philippines	1 Aug: Manuel Quezon, president of Philippine government in exile in US, dies of tuberculosis and is succeeded by Sergio Osmeña.
1945	Burma, Dutch Indies and Philippines	Japanese defeated; colonial regimes re-established in Burma, Malaya, Dutch Indies and Philippines.
	Indochina	2 Sep: Hồ Chí Minh proclaims Democratic Republic of Vietnam; French refuse to recognise this.

YEAR	HISTORY	CULTURE
1941	Second World War: Germany invades USSR. Japan attacks Pearl Harbor, invades the Philippines. Germany and Italy declare war on US. Atomic bomb development begins in USA.	Etienne Gilson, *God and Philosophy*. Bertold Brecht, *Mother Courage and Her Children*. Noel Coward, *Blithe Spirit*. Films: *Citizen Kane. Dumbo. The Maltese Falcon*.
1942	Second World War: US invasion of Guadalcanal turns Japanese tide. Battle of Stalingrad in USSR. Eisenhower lands in Morocco and Algeria.	Nobel Prize in Literature: No award. Dmitri Shostakovich, *Symphony No. 7*. Albert Camus, *The Outsider*. Film: *Casablanca*.
1944	Second World War: British and US forces in Italy liberate Rome. D-Day landings in France. Franklin D Roosevelt wins unprecedented fourth term as US President.	Carl Jung, *Psychology and Religion*. Michael Tippett, *A Child of Our Time*. Terrence Rattigan, *The Winslow Boy*. Tennessee Williams, *The Glass Menagerie*. Film: *Henry V*.
1945	Second World War: Yalta Conference. VE Day: 8 May. US drops atomic bombs on Hiroshima and Nagasaki: Japan surrenders to Allies. Twenty-nine nations ratify United Nations Charter.	Karl Popper, *The Open Society and its Enemies*. Benjamin Britten, *Peter Grimes*. George Orwell, *Animal Farm*. Film: *Brief Encounter*.

YEAR	COUNTRY	THE LIVES AND THE LANDS
1946	Thailand	9 Jun: King Ananda Mahidol is killed in obscure circumstances; he is succeeded by his younger brother Bhumibol Adulyadej.
	Philippines	4 Jul: Independence granted.
1948	Burma	4 Jan: Independence granted.
	Dutch Indies	31 Oct: Musso is killed, having returned to the Indies to lead an uprising.
1949	Dutch Indies	27 Dec: Independence granted as Republic of Indonesia.
1953	Indochina	9 Nov: Independence granted to Cambodia.
1954	Indochina	Independence granted to Laos; defeated at Điện Biên Phủ, France agrees at Geneva Conference to withdraw from Vietnam.
1975	Vietnam	30 Apr: With the capture of Saigon the division of Vietnam ends.

YEAR	HISTORY	CULTURE
1946	UN General Assembly opens in London. Churchill declares Stalin has lowered 'Iron Curtain' across Europe, signalling formal start of Cold War.	Nobel Prize in Literature: Hermann Hesse (Switzerland). Bertrand Russell, *History of Western Philosophy*. Eugene O'Neill, *The Iceman Cometh*. Film: *It's a Wonderful Life*.
1948	Gandhi assassinated in India: last British troops leave. Sri Lanka becomes self-governing.	Nobel Prize in Literature: T S Eliot (Great Britain). Graham Greene, *The Heart of the Matter*. Film: *Hamlet*.
1949	Mao Zedong establishes People's Republic of China.	Richard Rogers and Oscar Hammerstein, *South Pacific*.
1953	Stalin dies. Korean Armistice signed.	Arthur Miller, *The Crucible*. Film: *From Here to Eternity*.
1954	European Political Community Constitution drafted, later adopted. Anglo-Egyptian Agreement for British withdrawal from Canal Zone signed.	Benjamin Britten, *The Turn of the Screw*. Kingsley Amis, *Lucky Jim*. William Golding, *Lord of the Flies*. Film: *The Seven Samurai*.
1975	British vote 'Yes' in referendum on EEC membership. Indira Gandhi declares state of emergency in India.	Michel Foucault, *Discipline and Punish*. Queen, *Bohemian Rhapsody*. Film: *Jaws*.

Further Reading

South East Asia and the Peace Conference

The standard one-volume history of South East Asia has been D G E Hall, *A History of South-East Asia* (4th ed. Macmillan, London: 1981). Hall (1891–1979) was the youngest among the founding professors of the University of Rangoon in 1921. Much larger, important both for the chapters (with their resolutely regional approach) and the bibliographical essays, is Nicholas Tarling (ed), *The Cambridge History of Southeast Asia, vol. 2: the nineteenth and twentieth centuries* (Cambridge University Press, Cambridge: 1992). Note especially Chapter 3 by Reynaldo Ileto, 'Religion and anti-colonial movements', pp 193–244; and Chapter 4 by Paul Kratoska and Ben Batson, 'Nationalism and modernist reform', pp 245–320. In the 1999 reissue these chapters are in Vol 3. For some alternative views, Clive J Christie, A Modern History of Southeast Asia: decolonization, nationalism and separatism (Tauris, London: 1996).

Nicholas Tarling in *Imperialism in Southeast Asia: 'a fleeting, passing phase'* (Routledge, London: 2001) and in *Nationalism in Southeast Asia: 'if the people are with us'* (2004) offers two theoretically-inclined volumes with pithy insights into political events in the region. F R Mehden, *Religion and Nationalism in Southeast Asia* (University of Wisconsin Press, Madison: 1963) shows the special importance of religion in South East Asian politics. Charles B McLane, *Soviet Strategies in Southeast Asia: an exploration of eastern policy under Lenin and Stalin* (Princeton University Press, Princeton: 1966) explores early communist involvement in the region.

On Singapore and Malaya note C F Yong and R B McKenna, *The Kuomintang Movement in British Malaya 1912–1949* (Singapore University Press, Singapore: 1990); David Kenley, *New Culture in a New World: the May Fourth Movement and the Chinese diaspora in Singapore 1919–1932* (Routledge, London: 2003); also P Cavendish, 'Anti-Imperialism in the Kuomintang 1923–8' in Jerome Ch'en and Nicholas Tarling (eds), *Studies in the Social History of China and South-East Asia: essays in memory of Victor Purcell* (Cambridge University Press, Cambridge: 1970) pp 23–56.

J S Furnivall's *Colonial Policy and Practice: a comparative study of Burma and Netherlands India* (Cambridge University Press, Cambridge: 1948; 2nd ed., 1960) remains important. Furnivall (1878–1960) was present at the historic YMBA meeting in 1908 and became an innovative theorist of the 'plural societies' of colonial South East Asia.

Burma

John F Cady, *A History of Modern Burma* (Cornell University Press, Ithaca: 1958) is a thorough one-volume history of Burma in the 19th and 20th centuries. May Oung, speaker at the 1908 YMBA meeting, was the compiler of 'The Chronology of Burma' in *Journal of the Burma Research Society* Vol 2 (1912) pp 8–29.

The early years of Burmese nationalism are covered in Aye Kyaw, *The Voice of Young Burma* (SEAP Publications, Singapore: 1993) and in a work by U Maung Maung, *From Sangha to Laity: nationalist movements of Burma 1920–1940* (Manohar, New Delhi: 1980). This is well-documented and admirably unbiased. The sequel, *Burmese Nationalist Movements 1940–1948* (Kiscadale, Edinburgh: 1989) is equally important. *Robert H Taylor, The State in Burma* (Hurst, London: 1987) is also insightful. E M Mendelson, *Sangha and State in Burma: a study of monastic sectarianism and leadership* (Cornell University Press, Ithaca: 1975) deals with the close links between Buddhism and politics. U Tin Htway's 'The role of literature in nation building' in *Journal of the Burma Research Society* Vol 55, no 1–2 (1972) pp 19–46 is an important survey of the contribution of literature and the press to early Burmese nationalism.

Sir Reginald Craddock's *The Dilemma in India* (Constable, London: 1929) includes Chapter 11 (pp 109–29), 'The separate problem of Burma', a poignant reminder of how imperialists viewed the changes that were already taking place in Burma. On the Karens see San C Po, *Burma and the Karens* (Elliott Stock, London: 1928) and, recently, Mikael Gravers, 'The Karen making of a nation' in Stein Tønnesson and Hans Antlöv (eds), *Asian Forms of the Nation* (Routledge, London: 1996) pp 237–69.

The Philippines

For commentaries on the American period see Stanley Karnow, *In Our Image: America's empire in the Philippines* (Ballantine, New York: 1990), and Julian Go and Anne Foster (eds), *The American Colonial State in the Philippines: global perspectives* (Duke University Press, Durham, North Carolina: 2003).

On the period immediately following the American arrival, two recent books are particularly useful for their viewpoints on the early careers of Manuel Quezon and Sergio Osmeña. These are Michael Cullinane, *Ilustrado Politics: Filipino elite responses to American rule, 1898–1908* (Ateneo de Manila University Press, Manila: 2003) and Resil B Mojares, *The War Against the Americans: resistance and collaboration in Cebu, 1899–1906* (Ateneo de Manila University Press, Manila: 1999). For aspects of American involvement see also Michael P Onorato, *A Brief Review of American Interest in the Philippines and Other Essays* (Berkeley: 1968; expanded ed., Manila: 1972), and Roy Watson Curry, *Woodrow Wilson and Far Eastern Policy, 1913–1921* (New York: 1957).

The first Independence Mission is covered briefly in Honesto A Villanueva, 'The Independence Mission 1919: Independence Lies Ahead' in *Asian Studies* Vol 9 (1971) pp 282–306; more fully in Bernardita Reyes Churchill, *The Philippine Independence Missions to the United States 1919–1934* (National Historical Institute, Manila: 1983). David Joel Steinberg, *Philippine Collaboration in World War II* (University of Michigan Press, Ann Arbor: 1967) is a measured account of the Philippines under Japanese rule, focusing on questions of 'loyalty' and 'collaboration' without rushing to judgement.

Two members of the Independence Mission became political historians, and their work remains useful: Maximo M Kalaw, *The Development of Philippine Politics* (Oriental Commercial Co., Manila: [1927?]) and Rafael Palma, *Nuestra compaña por la independencia desde Taft hasta Harrison (1901–1921)* (Manila: 1923). On other main players see Vicente Albano Pacis, *President Sergio Osmena: a fully documented biography* (Phoenix Press, Quezon City: 1971), and William Gueraiche, *Manuel Quezon: les Philippines de la decolonisation a la democratisation* (Maisonneuve et Larose, Paris: [2004]). Francis Burton Harrison wrote *The Corner-Stone of Philippine Independence* (Century, New York: 1922) immediately after his term as Governor. His diaries from 1935 to 1944, published by himself (the manuscript does not survive) and re-edited with notes by Michael P Onorato under the title *Origins of the Philippine Republic* (Department of Asian Studies, Cornell University, Ithaca: 1974), include important discussions of earlier events, frequently quoting Quezon. On Harrison's work see also Napoleon J Casambre, 'The Response to Harrison's Administration in the Philippines, 1913–21' in *Asian Studies* Vol 7 (1969) pp 156–70, and Michael P Onorato, 'Governor General Francis Burton Harrison and his Administration: a re-appraisal' in *Philippine Studies* Vol 18 (1970) pp 178–86.

Indonesia

M C Ricklefs, *A History of Modern Indonesia since c. 1200* (Stanford University Press, Stanford: 2008) has reached its fourth edition; an alternative approach is Adrian Vickers, *A History of Modern Indonesia* (Cambridge University Press, Cambridge: 2005). Note also Chr L M Penders (ed), *Indonesia: selected documents on colonialism and nationalism 1830–1942* (University of Queensland Press, St Lucia: 1977).

Opposition to colonialism in early 20th century Indonesia is studied thoroughly, by way of the development of the communist movement, in Ruth McVey, *The Rise of Indonesian Communism* (Cornell University Press, Ithaca: 1965); also, more briefly, in Leslie Palmier, *Communists in Indonesia* (Weidenfeld and Nicolson, London: 1973). The trade union perspective is found in John Ingleson, *In Search of Justice: workers and unions in colonial Java, 1908–1926* (Oxford University Press, Singapore: 1986); that of religious reform and nationalism in Deliar Noer, *The Modernist Muslim Movement in Indonesia, 1900–1942* (Oxford University Press, Singapore: 1973). On this see also Chapter 3 (pp 56–90) of William R Roff's *The Origins of Malay Nationalism* (Yale University Press, New Haven: 1967; the 'second edition' [Oxford University Press, Kuala Lumpur: 1994] is a reissue). Note also Takashi Shiraishi, *An Age in Motion: popular radicalism in Java, 1912–1926* (Cornell University Press, Ithaca: 1990) and for the traditionalist background, from which several political leaders came, the detailed study by Romain Bertrand, *Etat colonial, noblesse et nationalisme à Java: la tradition parfaite* (Karthala, Paris: 2005). The origins of 'Indonesia', the modern incarnation of the Dutch Indies, are traced in R E Elson, *The Idea of Indonesia: a history* (Cambridge University Press, Cambridge: 2008).

Tony Saich, *The Origins of the First United Front in China: the role of Sneevliet (alias Maring)* (Brill, Leiden: 1991) is a collection of documents with an introductory survey of Sneevliet's activities until 1924 and with handy footnote biographies of his contacts. See also Michael Williams, 'Sneevliet and the Birth of Asian Communism' in *New Left Review* No 123 (Sep/Oct 1980). Semaun's historical sketch of Indies communism, presented in Moscow in 1922, is edited and translated by Ruth McVey as 'An Early Account of the Independence Movement', in *Indonesia* No 1 (April 1966) pp 46–75. Tan Malaka's memoirs are available as *From Jail to Jail*, translated by Helen Jarvis (Ohio University Center for International Studies, Athens, Ohio: 1991).

Vietnam

For a general history of the modern period see Joseph Buttinger, *Vietnam: a dragon embattled* (Praeger, New York: 1967). Note also William J Duiker, *Historical Dictionary of Vietnam* (Scarecrow, Metuchen: 1989).

The interplay between administration and resistance can be approached from several angles. For the resisters, see David Marr, *Vietnamese Anticolonialism 1885–1925* (University of California Press, Berkeley: 1971), with a special focus on the activities of Phan Bội Châu and Phan Chu Trinh; and its sequel, David G Marr, *Vietnamese Tradition on Trial, 1920–1945* (University of California Press, Berkeley: 1981), a well-told, very complex story; Hue-Tam Ho Tai, *Radicalism and the Origins of the Vietnamese Revolution* (Harvard University Press, Cambridge: 1992), focusing on Nguyễn An Ninh and other non-communist radicals of the 1920s. Christopher E Goscha, *Thailand and the Southeast Asian Networks of the Vietnamese Revolution, 1885–1954* (Curzon, Richmond: 1999) explores previously-neglected links with Siam. From the viewpoint of the colonial administration and the old empire, see Charles Fourniau, *Vietnam: domination coloniale et résistance nationale, 1858–1914* (Les Indes Savantes, Paris: 2002); Nguyên Thê Anh, *Monarchie et fait colonial au Viêt-n'm, 1875–1925: le crépuscule d'un ordre traditionnel* (L'Harmattan, Paris: 1992); and four increasingly detailed studies by Patrice Morlat: *La repression coloniale au Vietnam, 1908–1940* (L'Harmattan, Paris: 1990); *Les affaires politiques de l'Indochine, 1895–1923: les grands commis: du savoir au pouvoir* (L'Harmattan, Paris: 1995); *Indochine années vingt: le balcon de la France sur le Pacifique* (Les Indes Savantes, Paris: 2001) and *Indochine années vingt: le rendez-vous manqué, 1918–1928* (Les Indes Savantes, Paris: 2005). The last two are instalments of a formidable triptych on French Indochina in the 1920s, focusing throughout on the administration's aims, achievements and failures.

Albert Sarraut's writings included *La mise en valeur des colonies françaises* (Payot, Paris: 1923). Hồ Chí Minh (under the name Nguyễn Ái Quốc) published *Le procès de la colonisation française* (Librairie du Travail, Paris: 1925; new ed., Pantin: Le Temps des Cerises, 1999). For his life see William Duiker, *Ho Chi Minh* (Hyperion, New York: 2000); Sophie Quinn-Judge, *Ho Chi Minh: the missing years* (Hurst, London: 2003); more briefly, Pierre Brocheux, *Ho Chi Minh: a biography* (Cambridge University Press, Cambridge: 2007); and for documents on the Paris years, Thu Trang-Gaspard, *Hồ Chí Minh à Paris* (L'Harmattan, Paris: 1992). Phan-văn-Trường, *Une histoire de conspirateurs annamites à Paris* (Giadinh [i.e. Saigon]: 1928; new ed. by Ngo Van Xuyet: L'Insomniaque, Montreuil: 2003) is excellent if taken with a pinch of salt. On Phan Bội Châu see Vĩnh Sính (ed), *Phan Bội Châu and the Đông Du movement* (Yale Center for International and Area Studies, New Haven: 1988). There is now a sympathetic biography of Prince Cường Để: Trần Mỹ-Vân, *A Vietnamese Royal Exile in Japan: Prince Cường Để (1882–1951)* (Routledge, London: 2005). See also Agathe Larcher-Goscha, 'Prince Cuong Dê and the Franco-Vietnamese Competition for the Heritage of Gia Long' in *Viêt Nam Exposé: French scholarship on twentieth-century Vietnamese society* ed. Gisèle Luce Bousquet and Pierre Brocheux (University of Michigan Press, Ann Arbor: 2002) pp 187–215.

Siam

The most recent general history is Chris Baker and Pasuk Phongpaichit, *A History of Thailand* (Cambridge University Press, Cambridge: 2005); there is also David K Wyatt, *Thailand: a short history* (Yale University Press, New Haven: 2003).

On the last years of the absolute monarchy, see Benjamin A Batson, *The End of the Absolute Monarchy in Siam* (Oxford University Press, New York: 1984); Stephen L W Greene, *Absolute Dreams: Thai government under Rama VI, 1910–1925* (White Lotus, Bangkok: 1999) and Walter F Vella, *Chaiyo! King Vajiravudh and the Development of Thai Nationalism* (University Press of Hawaii, Honolulu: 1978). There are useful insights in Chula Chakrabongse, *Lords of Life: the paternal monarchy of Bangkok, 1782–1932* (Alvin Redman, London: 1960); this is a dynastic history by a nephew of Vajiravudh and Prajadhipok, and it includes discreet but revealing characterisations of these two monarchs and others. There is also a fascinating study of the early impulse to Westernise and 'civilise' Siam, Thongchai Winichakul, 'The Quest for "Siwilai": a geographical discourse of civilizational thinking in the late nineteenth and early twentieth-century Siam' in *Journal of Asian Studies* Vol 59 (2000) pp 528–49.

On the stirrings in Paris that preceded the 1932 revolution see Judith A Stowe, *Siam Becomes Thailand: a story of intrigue* (Hurst, London: 1991); and on two of the principal participants, Scot Barmé, *Luang Wichit Wathakan and the Creation of a Thai Identity* (Institute of Southeast Asian Studies, Singapore: 1993); Pridi Phanomyong, *Pridi by Pridi: selected writings on life, politics, and economy* ed. Chris Baker and Pasuk Phongpaichit (Silkworm Books, Bangkok: 2000).

Picture Sources

The author and publishers wish to express their thanks to the following sources of illustrative material and/or permission to reproduce it. They will make proper acknowledgements in future editions in the event that any omissions have occurred.

Courtesy of Getty Images and Topham Picturepoint.

Endpapers
The Signing of Peace in the Hall of Mirrors, Versailles, 28th June 1919 by Sir William Orpen (Imperial War Museum: akg Images)
Front row: Dr Johannes Bell (Germany) signing with Herr Hermann Müller leaning over him
Middle row (seated, left to right): General Tasker H Bliss, Col E M House, Mr Henry White, Mr Robert Lansing, President Woodrow Wilson (United States); M Georges Clemenceau (France); Mr David Lloyd George, Mr Andrew Bonar Law, Mr Arthur J Balfour, Viscount Milner, Mr G N Barnes (Great Britain); Prince Saionji (Japan)
Back row (left to right): M Eleftherios Venizelos (Greece); Dr Afonso Costa (Portugal); Lord Riddell (British Press);

Sir George E Foster (Canada); M Nikola Pašić (Serbia); M
Stephen Pichon (France); Col Sir Maurice Hankey, Mr Edwin
S Montagu (Great Britain); the Maharajah of Bikaner (India);
Signor Vittorio Emanuele Orlando (Italy); M Paul Hymans
(Belgium); General Louis Botha (South Africa); Mr W M
Hughes (Australia)

Jacket images
(Front): Imperial War Museum: akg Images.
(Back): *Peace Conference at the Quai d'Orsay* by Sir William
Orpen (Imperial War Museum: akg Images).
Left to right (seated): Signor Orlando (Italy); Mr Robert
Lansing, President Woodrow Wilson (United States); M
Georges Clemenceau (France); Mr David Lloyd George, Mr
Andrew Bonar Law, Mr Arthur J Balfour (Great Britain);
Left to right (standing): M Paul Hymans (Belgium); Mr
Eleftherios Venizelos (Greece); The Emir Feisal (The
Hashemite Kingdom); Mr W F Massey (New Zealand);
General Jan Smuts (South Africa); Col E M House (United
States); General Louis Botha (South Africa); Prince Saionji
(Japan); Mr W M Hughes (Australia); Sir Robert Borden
(Canada); Mr G N Barnes (Great Britain); M Ignacy
Paderewski (Poland)

Index

Makers of the Modern World

UK PUBLICATION: November 2008 to December 2010
CLASSIFICATION: Biography/History/
   International Relations
FORMAT: 198 × 128mm
EXTENT: 208pp
ILLUSTRATIONS: 6 photographs plus 4 maps
TERRITORY: world

Chronology of life in context, full index, bibliography innovative layout with sidebars

Woodrow Wilson: United States of America by Brian Morton
Friedrich Ebert: Germany by Harry Harmer
Georges Clemenceau: France by David Watson
David Lloyd George: Great Britain by Alan Sharp
Prince Saionji: Japan by Jonathan Clements
Wellington Koo: China by Jonathan Clements
Eleftherios Venizelos: Greece by Andrew Dalby
From the Sultan to Atatürk: Turkey by Andrew Mango
The Hashemites: The Dream of Arabia by Robert McNamara
Chaim Weizmann: The Dream of Zion by Tom Fraser
Piip, Meierovics & Voldemaras: Estonia, Latvia & Lithuania by Charlotte Alston
Ignacy Paderewski: Poland by Anita Prazmowska
Beneš, Masaryk: Czechoslovakia by Peter Neville
Károlyi & Bethlen: Hungary by Bryan Cartledge
Karl Renner: Austria by Jamie Bulloch
Vittorio Orlando: Italy by Spencer Di Scala
Pašić & Trumbić: The Kingdom of Serbs, Croats and Slovenes by Dejan Djokic
Aleksandŭr Stamboliĭski: Bulgaria by R J Crampton
Ion Bratianu: Romania by Keith Hitchin
Paul Hymans: Belgium by Sally Marks
General Smuts: South Africa by Antony Lentin
William Hughes: Australia by Carl Bridge
William Massey: New Zealand by James Watson
Sir Robert Borden: Canada by Martin Thornton
Maharajah of Bikaner: India by Hugh Purcell
Afonso Costa: Portugal by Filipe Ribeiro de Meneses
Epitácio Pessoa: Brazil by Michael Streeter
South America by Michael Streeter
Central America by Michael Streeter
South East Asia by Andrew Dalby
The League of Nations by Ruth Henig
Consequences of Peace: The Versailles Settlement – Aftermath and Legacy by Alan Sharp